I'M PRANCING AS FAST AS I CAN

Advance Praise for *I'm Prancing as Fast as I Can*

"I knew Jon Kinnally could make me laugh from years of working with him on *Will & Grace*, but I didn't know he could make me cry too. Dammit, Jon! What a beautiful, open hearted, hilarious book. If I were the kind of person who read a book a second time I would consider doing it with this one."

—Gary Janetti, *New York Times* bestselling author of *Do You Mind If I Cancel?*

"Like the greatest storytellers, Kinnally was able to make me laugh out loud on one page before ripping my heart out on the next. Hilarious, true, poignant, necessary! There isn't a person on earth (and maybe three or four other inhabited planets) that shouldn't read this book ASAP!"

—Blair Fell, author of the award-winning *The Sign For Home and Disco Witches of Fire Island*

"These stories are rich, and the one-liners are unforgettable!"

—Gabrielle Hamilton, *New York Times* bestselling author of *Blood, Bones, & Butter: The Inadvertent Education of a Reluctant Chef*

"Jon's gut-funny and heart-felt account of pushing himself to be straight in adolescence then finding his gay soulmate in New York City's vibrant, '80s art scene amidst the looming AIDS crisis is both poignant and triumphant. You'd have to be a myopic, fully clenched, elder Republic**t to deny yourself this read."

—Laura Kightlinger,
Stand-up comedian, writer.

"I've been friends with Jon forever so I can say this: Reading his book is like talking to that weird aunt you get stuck with at a family reunion only to discover she's the most interesting person there. Both hilarious and heartfelt—I loved it. Highly recommended!"

—Miss Coco

I'M PRANCING AS FAST AS I CAN

MY JOURNEY FROM A SELF-LOATHING CLOSET CASE TO A SUCCESSFUL TV WRITER WITH SOME SELF-ESTEEM

JON KINNALLY

PERMUTED PRESS

A PERMUTED PRESS BOOK
ISBN: 979-8-88845-950-8
ISBN (eBook): 979-8-88845-951-5

I'm Prancing As Fast As I Can:
My Journey From a Self-Loathing Closet Case to a Successful TV Writer With Some Self-Esteem

Cover design by Conroy Accord
Cover photo by Charlie Welch

All people, locations, events, and situations are portrayed to the best of the author's memory. While all of the events described are true, many names and identifying details have been changed to protect the privacy of the people involved.

Permuted Press
New York • Nashville
permutedpress.com

Published in the United States of America
1 2 3 4 5 6 7 8 9 10

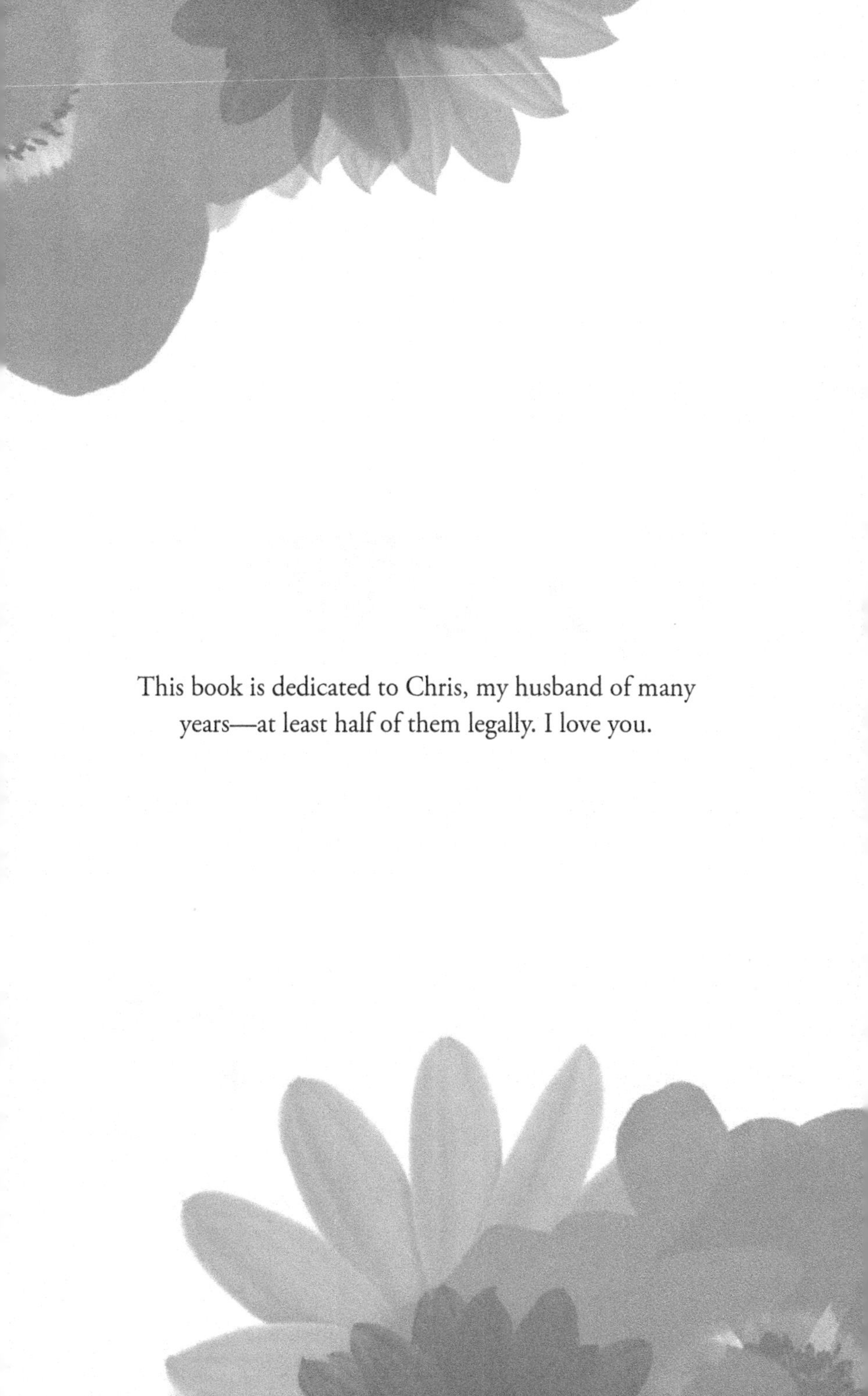

This book is dedicated to Chris, my husband of many years—at least half of them legally. I love you.

Table of Contents

Foreword

When I first met Jon Kinally, I thought he was straight. Mostly because his style felt more "lumberjack" than Jack McFarland. We wrote together on a show called *Daytime Divas* on VH1.

I mean, it was a good show, but I remember being confused as to why a writer on seminal shows like *Will & Grace* and *Ugly Betty* would end up writing for a television program on VH1. Did he spend all his money? Was he blacklisted by Hollywood?

He definitely spent all his money. He told me so while driving me home one night from work. (I have CP and can't drive. Jon has a car and apparently no friends.)* By that point, I knew Jon was gay. And I knew he was fucking funny. His wit somehow managed to be both caustic and a warm hug. Like we would say in the writers room for the *Will & Grace* reboot—the second job I worked on with Jon—it felt like "a kiss and a punch."

His essays in *I'm Prancing as Fast As I Can* are like that too. Since I am famously very young, I didn't understand a lot of the references. (Don't get mad but who is Betty Buckley, babe?) In

*Girl, are you trolling me in my own book??

a lot of ways, reading these vignettes feels like taking a trip on the gay Oregon trail—a time of payphones, of spontaneity, of life happening to you without an obsessive need to document it, although I'm sure happy Jon eventually did. Not to brag but I've fucked my fair share of old guys. Not Jon, although considering there's an entire chapter dedicated to him being a disability fetishist, it's a miracle he never tried to smash. My favorite part about putting the "ho" in hospice though is that, after they've come inside me, I get to hear stories about their lives. Stories like the ones in this book. Stories of losing your virginity at a truck stop (how retro!). Stories of finding yourself at a time when many people were losing themselves to AIDS. Jon's generation should be more hardened and calcified but they're not. There's a fragility there, sure, but also an openness and generosity.

What I found most interesting about these essays is the juxtaposition of the mundanity (trying to hook up with a flop, going on a lame acting audition) with the monumental (life at St. Vincent's hospital in the '80s and '90s, Jon's activism work with ACT UP!) Much has been written about living through AIDS. What isn't discussed as much is all the daily humiliations of being alive that were still happening in the background. You were still trying to get laid. You were still trying to buy coke at a house party. You still were unsure how to mail something. Jon's excellent at giving space for both. One standout story "Spanking The Cat" starts off as a love letter to—who else?—his cat and then quickly morphs into a stunning retelling of losing his partner to leukemia. Jon's superpower is that he hides the vegetables in sugar. He's fucking hilarious, obviously—joke, joke, joke—but then, like a sniper, he hits you with a deep, emotionally resonant truth. "I know shit," Jon screams on ketamine in the intro to this collection. I guess he does...

A lot has changed since Jon came of age. He writes lovingly about his divas (Madonna, Tina Turner, a random blind girl he met at school) because he didn't have actual gay role models.

Jon would go on to help shape the role models himself for the next generation via his writing on *Will & Grace*. I remember being twelve and seeing someone as faggy as Jack McFarland on TV for the first time. "Hmmm," I thought. "Maybe I'm not so weird for walking around the house with a T-shirt on my head I like to call 'My Mary.'" In order to be yourself, you have to see yourself.

Thanks to Jon, I was able to start coloring myself in.

But I do have one bone to pick with Jon. In the intro, he posits that suffering is integral to character-building, that Generation PrEP got off scot-free by not having to bury friends every weekend, that Millennials and Gen Z don't know the gay men who came before them. (Or, in my case, on them.) If you didn't ever have to hate yourself, how can you appreciate anything?

Don't worry, Jon. People will always find new, modern ways to hate themselves. Shame is an heirloom passed on through every generation. I grew up with supportive parents and a gay uncle and I still thought, "You've got to be fucking kidding me..." the first time I came to Ryan Phillippe's ass in *Cruel Intentions*. That's why we will always need essays like the ones in this book. Essays that call out shame and diffuse its power through humor and radical honesty.

Essays that don't shy away from the ugliness of life and the attempts to make it beautiful.

Essays that dive into the pain of folding yourself into smaller parts, Origami-style, because you're scared of making your presence big.

These stories are a balm in a sick time. Betty Buckley, an American actress, singer, two-time Daytime Emmy and Grammy award-winner would've loved them. (There, Jon. I Googled her. You happy now?!) (Postscript: Oh, wait. She's still alive. I meant, "She will love them!")

Ryan O'Connell
Creator of Netflix's *Special*

Introduction

"Everything in this room is so beige—beige couch, beige rug, beige walls, who knew there were so many shades of beige?" I babbled nervously as my psychiatrist jabbed the needle in my arm. I had started ketamine therapy because why not? Dolphin therapy seemed too expensive. And I felt like I already owed them, having one or two push me across a pool at a tacky resort with their snouts on my feet. They acted like they were fine, but I could tell they hated it. And I felt like an asshole doing it.

People are taking ketamine (Special K to the club kids!) as a way of fighting depression. It's an all-purpose drug: It's good for dancing (though too much can send you into a "k-hole"), it's a horse tranquiliser, and it's a human anesthetic. And, apparently, it's also something people will spend a lot of money to do so they can trip balls in their shrink's office in Marina del Rey.

As the ketamine kicked in, I experienced the classic "We are all one/None of this is real/*Matrix*" kind of shit. I saw my mother shopping at the grocery store. I saw monkeys shopping at the grocery store. I returned to the Sacred Monkey Forest in Bali, where I went twenty years ago with my then-boyfriend, Gecko (he had HIV and, as a monkey climbed on his shoulders,

I told him that he should bite it and get his revenge). It was pretty cool, like looking through a kaleidoscope on acid. Or ketamine. And then, suddenly, I was seized by the most intense of truths, and I yelled out, "You *know* shit!" Then I yelled, "Write that down!"

My shrink and I discussed what I shouted when I came down from my trip. He seemed to think the phrase, "You *know* shit!" was about him, the smug bastard. But I'm pretty sure I was talking about myself. I let him think what he wanted—it was better than getting into a whole thing with him.

"You *know* shit!"

I know shit.

This phrase stayed with me as I was starting back in the writer's room on the reboot of *Will & Grace*. There was a new young writer on staff, and we got to talking, as gays do. And since he had precious, precious youth, I was forced to make myself superior to him with the only tool I had—the wisdom that supposedly comes with age.

When I steered the conversation to Gay history, he stopped me and said he knew all about Stonehenge.

Stone*henge*.

I would've done a spit take if I wasn't wearing my favorite vintage-looking Todd Snyder top. I quietly, but with great import, explained to him that StoneWALL was the name of the Gay bar in New York where, on the night of July 28th, 1969—several hours after Judy Garland's funeral—the police raided yet again. Only this time the Gays, Lesbians, Transgenders, and drag queens fought back. A Lesbian somehow pulled up a parking meter and threw it through a window, as Lesbians do. And thus, the modern Gay rights movement was born. Or at least took a giant leap forward.[1]

I'm sure I had the right amount of indignation and condescension in my voice as I schooled this youngling—or at least I do in the retelling. But he didn't really give a shit. I may know shit, but he didn't. And he was fine with that.

Still, I tried to teach him about his history. Oscar Wilde. The meaning of the pink triangle during World War II. Did he even know about groups like ACT UP? Did he know about the struggle to fight AIDS and the efforts to get life-saving drugs approved quicker to help the people who were dying? Did he?!

Arguably as important—because I say it is—had he seen the '70s John Travolta TV movie, *The Boy in the Plastic Bubble*? And did he identify with John, who lived his life unable to touch anyone? Did he understand the need for secrecy and double lives?

In *his* youth, he could just say, "I don't want to play in Little League." Did he understand that we didn't have that option in the not-too-distant past? Did he realize that many of us felt compelled to play and prayed to God—the same god who

1 Of course there are many important events in Gay history, including the demonstration against police brutality at The Black Cat in LA in 1967 and the 1966 riot at Compton's Cafeteria in San Francisco in response to police harassment of Trans people and drag queens. Also, the incident outside the Eagle on Twenty-Eighth Street in New York in 1992, when, as I drunkenly stumbled out of the bar, I was called a "faggot ass fag" by men who sped by in a Kia. I cleverly yelled "Fuck you" at the retreating car, moving the Gay cause just that much forward. The list goes on and on.

disapproved of us—that the coach would put us so far in left field that the ball couldn't come anywhere near us?[2]

When he was still a pre-tween, he might have been able to say to his parents, "Nick Jonas is so cute!" Chances are he would never relate to me riding my bike to the woods behind the school and shamefully jerking off to the picture of the guy's back on the Doan's pill box, praying God and my dead grandfather weren't watching.[3] Gay history!

HE DIDN'T EVER HAVE TO HATE HIMSELF!

I worry about this generation in which Gay is okay (well, mostly okay). Where will the art come from? Where will the comedy come from? It often comes from suffering. From taking horrible moments and adding a bit of nostalgia and exaggeration and making it something that a certain generation could relate to and laugh at.

I said this to him, and all I got in return was, "Stop flirting with me—we will never fuck."

But I wasn't flirting with him—well, I was—but mostly I was trying to *inform* him. To make him appreciate what he had and how he got it. And I know for a *fact* that people love to be informed and forced to appreciate stuff—especially by someone with attitude and a sense of superiority.

Yes, he owes Alexander the Great and President Lincoln (read the letters!) and President Buchanan (the "Bachelor President")

---

2 I've decided to Capitalize "God" and use "he/him" a few times because it helps me access the horror of growing up Catholic and believing this angry man would drag me to hell for thinking impure thoughts about our local priest, Father Bear. Yes, that was his name. And, yes, that's what he was.

3 You'll hear more about the man on the box of Doan's Pills. He is actually a drawing of a man, mostly seen from the back, which he is clutching in pain. It makes sense because the pills are for back pain. He was my best friend, my lover, and my confidant. He was there at a time when I needed him and I will be eternally grateful. Sadly, I could never take his pain away. It was kinda his thing.

and Audra Lorde and Gertrude Stein and the Mattachine Society and James Baldwin and Barney Frank and the Hate Crimes Prevention Act and much, much more for the rights he enjoys today.

But he also owes me.

I didn't suffer under Henry VIII's Buggery Act of 1533, which made homosexuality punishable by death, but in my journey through the last few decades—since that preternaturally strong Lesbian threw that parking meter—I did survive many micro versions of it that helped him get to that seat next to me. Fuck "Stonehenge," he needed to know about *them*.

In case things go tits up again, he might need to know shit.

And as established:

I *know* shit.

Keep On Truckin'[4]

I was a teenage sex worker on Thanksgiving.

I was fourteen. And tired of being a virgin. Well, really, I was tired of struggling with the idea that I might not be entirely heterosexual. I would sit on my top bunk and stare sadly at my Farrah Fawcett poster for hours in a sweaty panic:[5] *Why don't I have sexy feelings for you?! Why do I have them for the man holding his back in pain on the box of Doan's pills in the medicine cabinet? That can't be good, right?!* And the clock was ticking. At fourteen, if the feelings weren't there, they probably weren't going to come without taking some kind of action. I could no longer be considered a late bloomer.

To make matters worse, I looked older than my age. Of course, it didn't help that I was sporting a pretty respectable mustache. Earlier that year, my mom bought me a T-shirt that read, "MUSTACHE RIDES 25 CENTS." I was mortified. She

4 In the late '60s, "Keep On Truckin'" was a popular subject in poster art created by R. Crumb, a countercultural artist who founded *Weirdo Magazine*, one of the most prominent publications of the alternative comics era.

5 Farrah Fawcett was one of the original *Charlie's Angels*. Her poster with her famous hair and red one piece was on every boy's wall in the late '70s, giving the parents of Gay boys hope. I also had a poster of punk rock priestess Patti Smith showing her hairy armpits which probably confused mine. I know it confused me.

feigned ignorance to the sexual message, but I knew what she was thinking: *My son made the family watch* A Star is Born *the other night—the Barbra Streisand version. Drastic action is called for.* And she was right, it was. It was.

It wasn't as if I didn't *want* a girlfriend. More accurately, I wanted to want one. But I just didn't know what that involved. Literally. When my friends would talk about going out with this girl or that girl, I would wonder: *What does that even mean? What do they talk about on these "outings?" And who could I even ask to find out?*

You needed to know things. How far to go, for example. By that point, I had kissed a lot of girls, including a make out session with Connie Dimarco that felt like it went on for days. I was having an okay time, but I knew what she was thinking: *Why doesn't he touch my boobs?* But I was thinking: *I'm kinda content with what we are doing now.* And what worked in my favor? The fact that Connie was too embarrassed to move things to the next level. Thank god for the patriarchy!

I mean, girls were called "sluts" for wanting to go "further." And sometimes just called "sluts" for no reason at all. I remember the rumors about Janet Minor in high school. If you believed what was said about her, she had blown almost all the guys on the lacrosse team and had once stuck a hotdog "up herself." That part really confused me. I had imagined a sort of vaginal shelf where things were stored and often forgotten about. We weren't very woke—or knowledgeable—then.

So, I needed some experience. And I needed it fast. I had read *The Catcher in the Rye* and had seen enough movies to know that the best way to get it was to hire a prostitute (it was still the early '80s—they weren't "sex workers" yet).[6] A prostitute wouldn't complain if I couldn't perform. Or if I prematurely ejaculated. She'd probably be relieved. She'd think: *Thank god! Now I can go have a cigarette with the other girls and laugh about what just happened.* And let her! Let her laugh at me. Let her have some fun in her life. In a way, my failure would be a positive thing. Maybe she'd spend the time I saved her relaxing wherever hookers gathered (they were also called "hookers" then). I imagined it being a dirty garage where they sat on crates. She'd put her feet up, light a cigarette, and tell her other smoking hooker companions, "Well, another faggot thought I could turn him. God bless those dumbass queers." I imagined the laughter all around. And then the coughing fits that would follow.

I decided "Project Prostitute" would happen on Thanksgiving Day because why not? We ate early. We always did. It was more like a really heavy lunch. My grandmother would come over. I loved my grandmother. At least, I did until many years later when I discovered that she was extremely racist. She would say the most awful things to the attendants who looked after her in the nursing home that she went to when she was too old to live alone with her racist thoughts. Her face would get mean and hard, and she'd say a bit too loud, "There's a Black one." Needless to say, I was horrified. Sometimes it can be terrible to learn the truth about people.

I remember sitting next to her at the table that Thanksgiving. I caught her staring at me. Even through the cataracts, I could see she knew what I was planning to do after lunch/dinner. She was probably just praying I did it with a white one.

6 *The Catcher in the Rye* is a great book. If you haven't already, read it. Fun game: I've stolen a line from it, see if you can find it!

My plan was simple. If I could "do it" with a woman, I would definitely be straight. Begin as you mean to go on, as they say. And all those pesky fantasies about Tom Selleck would just be memories my wife and I would laugh at as we dressed for a dinner party with our successful hetero friends.[7]

I spent a long time grooming for the event. I remember being bummed about several new zits that were changing the topography of my face. I used my father's electric razor so I could look good for the lucky, lucky prostitute who was to deflower me. But with zits like mine, the razor basically turned my face into a crime scene. To finish my grooming, I splashed on some aftershave, silently screaming into the bathroom mirror. A lot of silent things happened in that bathroom.

I left as soon as I could, lying that I was going to my friend Mark's house. "Bye, Honey!" my mother probably said from the kitchen as she silently seethed at my father for not helping her clean up. Under my jacket was a bottle of banana liqueur I had stolen from the cupboard. It was my mother's favorite booze, and she would save it for special occasions. When guests came over, she'd get a look in her eye that said: *Let's be bad*, and then she'd ask me to get the bottle, which she kept behind the good, unused china.

Motel 6 was about a mile from my house, near the off-ramp of Route 81. I didn't have much to compare the place to, but even I knew a motel with a number wasn't going to be glamorous. And it didn't disappoint. The desk clerk looked tired. He had a comb-over he didn't bother combing over anymore, like

---

7 Tom Selleck starred in *Magnum, P.I.*—a '70s TV series (remade since then). He was extremely sexy and always wore short shorts and frequently-open Hawaiian shirts, showing off his manly, hairy chest. Tom was very busy, as he also starred in many young boys' dreams.

it just wasn't worth the energy these days. I remember my room had a nondescript painting tightly secured to the wall. I found that odd, but what did I know? Maybe a lot of art thieves who specifically target boring landscapes covered in a grimy layer of cigarette smoke often stayed there.

It must have seemed weird to Comb-Over that I wasn't a gacked-out trucker like the rest of his guests. But I had given myself a cover story. I was traveling through town on my way to New York City for a *business* meeting—remember I looked older than I was. As he counted the bills I pushed at him, I briefly panicked. What if he asked what *kind* of business? I decided I'd say, "finance," and then cut any further chitchat short with, "I'm sorry, but I've really got to make an important call to the Coast," and impatiently hold out my hand for the key. As I walked away, I was a little disappointed he didn't care enough to ask. Or care that I didn't have luggage. I got mad at myself for not thinking of bringing a briefcase. Was I trying to sabotage this whole thing?!

I sat on the bed for about an hour, drinking what was left of the banana liqueur and trying to psych myself up. I had noticed earlier that the parking lot was full of trucks, and I strongly suspected that's where the action happened. Or at least got started. Finally, I made the decision. It was time. I checked to make sure the condoms were safely in the drawer where I put them earlier and left the room for the parking lot. I strolled around, trying to seem as casual as I could: *Nothing weird here, just a businessman taking the air and stretching his legs amongst the big wheelers. Darn it, why does that shoelace keep coming untied, forcing me to prolong my stroll and kneel and look around while I secured it again and again?*

I saw exactly no one. But in my mind, all the people who weren't there were somehow staring at me, wondering what the fuck I was doing. Where were the hookers?! Were they all on break? If so, I couldn't help but think they should stagger their breaks so they don't miss out on someone. It was a bad business plan. Even I—a fake businessman—could figure that out. I was frustrated on two levels: There were no women. And there was no place to take my grievance slash business advice to.

Finally, after tying my shoe for what must've been the fortieth time, I gave up and went to the bar. To feel older, I ordered coffee. To stay in character, I pretended to have lots of business type thoughts in my head: *Would I land the Larrabee account? Should I fire my secretary for being indiscrete?* I took a sip of my coffee and almost spit it out. It turned out I was so deep in my thoughts, I had put salt in it instead of sugar. The bartender gave me a sideways smirk, cigarette hanging out of his mouth, ash falling in the ice. I decided to return his look and keep drinking it so there was no doubt in either one of our minds that a mistake had not been made. *That's right, I'm a salty coffee–drinking businessman. I am not to be fucked with.*

Several cups later, I was hyped up from the caffeine and thirsty as fuck. And I was starting to freak out. It was getting late. And there was a lot riding on this. It felt like I was at a crossroads and if I didn't make it with a hooker at this truck stop on this night, I might never be saved. I barely made it back to my room before the tears came. Followed by the prayers. I wondered how often God received a prayer for a parking lot full of hookers.

I ventured back for another walkabout but still saw no one. In my memory, it started to rain. But I might have just added that at some later point to up the pathetic factor. Sadly, it became clear to me that nothing was going to happen. God did not answer my prayers. He may have been insulted or amused by them, but either way, I wasn't getting VD that night. (That's what we called STIs then. Also, that's what we used to associate with sex workers. That and glitter "boob tubes.")[8]

But then, suddenly, a ray of light broke through the made-up clouds, and I didn't feel alone in that parking lot. I turned to notice a burly man swigging a can of beer while leaning against a truck. He was watching me. We locked eyes for what must've been a nano second, but it was long enough for some kind of shift to happen that I couldn't explain. He made a small gesture with his head for me to follow him. And what do you do when a burly trucker in an empty parking lot gestures for you to follow him? You follow him. It would be rude not to.

I guessed the truck he was leaning against was his because he opened the door and climbed up into the cab. I remember hesitating, and he gave me a look that said: *What do you want, a fuckin' written invitation?* (remember—the 'stache added a few years to me) I climbed up onto the seat beside him. The cab smelled like air freshener trying to cover armpit and failing badly at it. *Why am I doing this?* I thought to myself. *I could be killed. They'll find my body behind the Motel 6 with the garbage and unclaimed luggage. Maybe the hookers will find it when they get off their break. They'll immediately know what happened with that wise, psychic sense that all hookers have.*

My heart was beating a mile a minute, my mind was racing. I wondered what he was hauling in his truck—was it Coke?—my dad worked for the Coke plant in Solvay—loading trucks—maybe they knew each other—I probably shouldn't ask him. I

8 I think you can figure this one out on your own.

mentally babbled. But eventually, something about him put me at ease. Maybe it was the fact that, in his trucker hat, beard, and flannel shirt, he was a walking cliché of what everyone thought a trucker should look like. Or maybe it was the feeling that he knew this but just didn't give a shit. I didn't have much time to debate this as he jumped right in and we started making out. Well, he started, and I caught up quickly. Again, it seemed rude not to.

We made out hard for a bit and then he unzipped my pants. And I let him. A part of me was thinking: *Stop him, this isn't the plan at all! It's very much the opposite of the plan!* But another part of me was thinking: *Oh, shut up, and let the nice trucker blow you. It's fun!* That part won. By a landslide.

Afterwards, my trucker smiled at me. He seemed different, like someone who wouldn't kill me at all. And then he said, "How much?" I have to say I was caught off guard by this. But only for a moment. "Twenty bucks," I was surprised to hear myself say. Where the fuck had that person come from? Maybe I really *was* a businessman. He took a twenty out of his wallet. Then, after a beat, he took out another and handed me both. Not only did he not kill me, but he tipped me generously!

The walk home was not the joyous one I had hoped. The night didn't prove I was straight. But it also didn't *necessarily* mean I was Gay. Maybe I was just "Gay for pay." Or at the very least I was bi which wasn't preferable, but was something I could work with. There was still hope! And if it was good enough for David Bowie, it was good enough for me.

Whew, it felt so good to have all that cleared up.

Tits On A Bull

A few years ago, my husband, Chris, and I went on a trip to Kauai. We stayed in a cottage on a former coffee plantation where the '70s miniseries *The Thorn Birds* was filmed. And, yes, the first thing we did was recreate the scene on the front porch where Barbara Stanwyck—the matriarch of the plantation—makes the rain-soaked priest, Richard Chamberlain, take off his wet clothes while she lewdly eyes him up and down. It's a very sexy, powerful scene and, frankly, in my opinion, it would've been weird if we *hadn't* honored it. The locals may have felt differently but we thought: *Fuck 'em.* We'll tip heavily when we check out.

The next day, while tooling around the island, we stopped at a botanical garden. We paid the entrance fee and bought five dollars' worth of bird feed, only to find ourselves physically assaulted by several different species of birds immediately upon entering. Basically, we were in the middle of a frenzied bird gang bang. Except for the peacocks. Those beautiful boys didn't have to do anything except let their plumage loose, and we came to them, humbled, our hands held out dripping with seeds and whatever other garbage filler they put in those bags. They would simply shimmy their beautiful feathers, making a sound like a rainstorm, and we would drop everything at their feet. I think I even left a pack of matches from where we were staying with my name and cottage number written on it.

It was amazing to us that something so beautiful, so resplendent, could exist. And that it was a male. Sorry, ladies, but the peahens are plain. I hope god gave them a great personality and a sense of humor.

We were also happy because it upset the "natural" order of things. It reminded me of something my mother used to say to me, "Jon, you're about as handy as tits on a bull." And for a long time, I wasn't sure what she meant exactly. I knew it was a put down, of course. And I really didn't mind that. It meant she was paying attention to me. Which was always nice. And I knew she wasn't saying it because she didn't like me. It was just a thing she said. Like "Jumping horse balls!" or "Your father is a lazy son of a bitch. Just sits on that couch all day, never does a goddamn thing!" I came to love the phrase. If you're going to be called useless, at least it's nice to have it done in an interesting, descriptive way.

And then one day, when I had grown a bit and was forced by bullies to discover the quiet safety of the library, I figured it out. *Tits on a bull.* That didn't make sense because bulls wouldn't have tits, not the kind my mother meant.

Later, looking back on it, I wondered: *Was she unconsciously picking up on something about me? Was I being Gay bashed by my own mother? Is it Gay bashing when the one hurling the homophobic insult doesn't know that's what it is and the one on the receiving end doesn't even know he's Gay yet?* For the sake of victimhood let's say, "yes."

Anyway, none of these deep questions mattered when I was a kid. In spite of my desperate need to feel "normal," I quietly wore her possibly homophobic slur like a badge of honor. Because I figured a bull with breasts would be a special bull. A bull who felt different. Like me. I secretly identified with this "freakish" bull. Much in the way I identified with the bull in the children's book *Ferdinand the Bull,* in which Ferdinand would rather smell flowers all day than fight.

But as I grew, I sadly realized that I was going to have to leave Ferdinand behind and conform to what everyone expected of me. And that did not involve smelling flowers. Or fucking with gender.

I have a confession to make. I used to be dragphobic. And I'm not proud of that. There was a time when I liked my men to be men and my women to be women. I was so young and stupid.

It was 1990, and drag was really taking off. But I thought it was sort of silly. And frivolous. But I kept my feelings to myself because I knew they weren't "PC" in the Gay circles I traveled in. I pretended to have nothing but respect for the Gay guys I knew who would dress up in heels and wigs and march in various parades and demonstrations. But secretly, I used to think: *Is this really the message we want to send to the world?* I worried about CNN putting the Radical Faeries or the Sisters of Perpetual Indulgence front and center, as if to say "Look at the freakshow!"[9] I wanted Gays to be represented by normal, cute,

[9] The Radical Faeries are a countercultural movement that rejects the hetero-imitative, commercialized, and patriarchal aspects of modern LGBTQ+ life. They are all about community, spirituality, and sexuality. It doesn't matter what your body type or age is, you are sexy AF to them! And you can pick a new name for yourself, often something having to do with nature or spirit. At the gathering I went to, I chose to call myself Mulch. The Sisters of Perpetual Indulgence are a charitable, protest, and street performance group of Gay guys decked out in glamor nun drag, sometimes on roller skates. If I was one, I would call myself Sister Mulch.

thin guys and girls. You know, the kind of folks who live next door—if the folks next door looked like people in the cigarette ads of my youth: playing tennis or shopping for produce in an open-air market, their lung cancer as yet undetected.

Yes, I knew that we owed drag queens an enormous debt. They were on the front lines at the Stonewall riots and stuff, and in doing so are directly responsible for the rights and freedoms I enjoy today, blah blah blah, but what had they done for me *lately*?

Was it my mother's comment? Was it the fact that I was sure, with my deep-set eyes, I would look terrible in daytime makeup? Was it my worry that drag seemed inherently misogynistic? Was it internalized homophobia?

Naturally, I wanted to blame the Catholic Church, which I grew up in. I'm not sure if there is an official doctrine on drag, but it doesn't seem a stretch to think of them as not being cool with it. Even though they wear caftans, which are the most forgiving of the feminine garments.

I also believe my brother might have had a hand in my problem.

When we were kids, a surefire way for him to get me to do anything was to threaten me with a training bra. I remember listening, horrified, as he explained to me what a training bra was: a bra that trained a young girl to grow boobs. And if a boy wore it, it didn't matter, he'd grow boobs too. This made perfect sense to me, and from then on, I was in his control. No matter what he wanted, he could get it with the simple threat: "Training bra."

First, he told me he would use one of my sister's bras. Then when she no longer needed one—when I guess her boobs were trained to do all the tricks they were going to do—he told me he stole one from her and kept it somewhere just for me. I searched and searched the house but never found it. "I'm going to get that training bra and put it on you," he would threaten, "and then you're going to grow boobs. Boobs!" As if that were the worst thing in the world. Now, a bull sniffing a flower was one thing, but being forced to physically change when I was already confused was too much to bear.

I didn't know then what I know now: if we are lucky enough to grow old then we're probably all going to have them. Old age is the great equalizer. And as a wise woman once never said but should have, "Whatever your ethnicity, color, orientation, or gender—we all look like midwestern Lesbians in the end." And I think that's kind of nice—a bringing together if you will. But at that young, stupid age, I was terrified. I had nightmares of waking up in a bathtub of ice. Except instead of a missing kidney, they had given me breasts. How would I hide them in gym?

Oddly, I had my epiphany (which come to think of it, would make a great drag name, Epiphany!) in the most terrifying of places: The Deep South.

It was a dismal Gay bar somewhere in Mississippi. With the kind of name they all have: "RUMORS," or "SECRETS," or "WHISPERS." Apparently, the queens loved to talk in hushed tones. I think we drove around the block several times until we realized it was indeed the boarded up burned out looking storefront on the corner. We entered in the back and were delighted to find we were just in time for the show. A drag show in a tacky Gay bar in a small town in Mississippi promised to be low rent and delicious.

And suddenly there she was, a vision in an '80s spandex dress that ruffled out at the bottom. I'll never forget her name: Ashley Outfit. And it seemed to suit her. She wasn't exactly cutting edge in her style, but her quiet dignity gave her a refinement in spite of her seven press-ons and Tammy Faye wig.[10] And she held onto that dignity as she lip-synched "The Wind Beneath My Wings" to the few dozen people in the cramped, smoky space. She faltered only once: when the dove she had carefully taken out of its cage got its claw twisted in the beading on her décolletage, forcing her to almost miss the cue while she untangled it. But she made it, and as she triumphantly sang—well, fake sang—the inspirational ending imploring her lover to "fly high against the sky," she released that dove, and we were rapt. Of course, the poor bird could only fly up about two or three feet before it hit the low ceiling and came to land somewhat shaken on the bar, feathers flying around it. But it didn't matter. Miss Outfit had us in the palm of her large hand, and we got the message she was imparting to us. Freedom. Not necessarily for the dazed and sickly bird but for all outsiders. For anyone who wanted to feel okay about themselves, even if it meant changing into a Goodwill dress in your car and putting on stolen supermarket makeup in a filthy men's room in order to go from peahen to peacock. Or was it peacock to peahen? Either way, I want to say thank you to her, because after I was Ashley Outfitted, I got it. I understood.

[10] Tammy Faye Bakker was a televangelist with her (probably Gay, definitely a criminal) husband Jim. She was known for her eccentric and camp-glamor persona, as well as for moral views that her peers didn't quite share, such as her advocacy for LGBTQ+ people and reaching out to HIV/AIDS patients at the height of the AIDS epidemic. She wore giant shoulder pads and a shit-ton of makeup that she became famous for crying off. Her husband went to jail for his crimes and she became a Gay icon.

And I returned to New York a full-on drag hag.[11] I envied the work they put in. The commitment involved. The in-your-face-ness of it! I rediscovered my Ferdinand.

I surrendered to my newfound drag haggery. For a while, I became the straight man to drag queens. Not sure how many men can say they let Miss Carriage strip them down on stage at the Pyramid on Avenue A and dump a can of beans down their Calvin's.[12] Hopefully not many. But maybe just enough to start a support group.

Oddly, it took future freak show and the Crypt Keeper's less attractive brother, Rudolph Giuliani, to coax me fully out of the drag closet. At some point in his ignoble career as mayor, he decided the Gay Pride Parade should be moved from Fifth Avenue, where it had been since its inception in 1969, to First Avenue, which made it easier for traffic but a lot more invisible to the public. Well, once again, the drag queens took over and refused to give in. I will never forget how powerful I felt marching down Fifth Avenue in the outlaw parade wearing Doc Martens, a short sundress, a red wig, and a big floppy hat, holding a cardboard machine gun that read "Warning—I fight like a girl." I'd like to think Ashley Outfit would have approved, but she probably would've thought I was pure trash.

Drag is power. Of course, there are those who will always come for it, but they will never stop the power of a Shake-N-Go wig and the freedom it represents. That glitter ain't ever going back in the glitter tube. Drag will survive and thrive, thanks to

11 "Drag Hag" is a spin on a much-maligned phrase that we will get to. Though in this case, it is not used to denigrate women and is therefore fine IMHO.

12 The Pyramid was a skanky club on Avenue A where I spent an unhealthy amount of time in the early '90s. I think it's closed now, but I'm sure there's the ghost of an old drag queen wandering around it, lip-synching to a song only she can hear.

such proud queens as Coco Peru, RuPaul, Lady Gaga, Debbie Harry, Timothée Chalamet, and Pope Francis—or as his close friends know him, Pope Fancy.

And I predict it will continue to spread.

One day soon, a big hairy man teetering on heels and wearing an ill-fitting slip dress from a dirty vintage store will no longer turn a head. It's a little sad in a way, but progress often is.

I imagine a time when everyone gets to dress however they feel. When women, men, children, and all other categories discover their inner drag queen. Maybe it even becomes a badge in scouting. People will know their shoe sizes in boys' and girls'. And they will get to choose a fun name for themselves, for their drag persona. Perhaps "Katrina Victims," who I imagine wears a souvenir T-shirt from the Superdome and is always soaking wet. Or "June Gloom," who always seems to be in a funk and never knows what weather to dress for. For the drag kings, maybe a "Hugh Briss," who would present as a very cocky Jewish entertainer. Or a drunk and sloppy "Rock Bottom."

For me, it will always be the simple but classic heels, wig, and boa, which can pretty much take you anywhere.

A wise man once never said but should have, "One can't truly become a man until he has walked a mile in stilettos and a bustier."

Sorry, Mom—tits on a bull may not be useful, or even attractive, but they can be empowering.

What Penguins Can Teach Us

My penguin made Betty Buckley cry. And that's not a statement many people can make. It happened in an acting class I was taking at the T. Schreiber Studio on Fourth Street in the East Village in the early '90s.[13]

Betty, star of stage, screen, and TV's *Eight Is Enough*, was teaching the concept of better acting through meditation. All you needed to bring was an open mind and a pillow to sit on. And she was a great teacher too. A little batty in the way that Broadway divas tend to be, but effective.

One week, our assignment was to act like an animal for the class. An animal that really meant something to us. We were to silently observe it for a week. Study it and make notes. We were encouraged to "*become*" the animal. I chose a penguin at the Central Park Zoo. Now there were a lot of penguins in the Penguin House at the Central Park Zoo, and I had to make sure I studied the same one each time, so I picked one with a

[13] *Eight Is Enough* was a mediocre TV series from the '70s about a man, his eight kids, and their new stepmother, Betty Buckley. Of course, the Gays wasted no time in making a porn called *Eight Is Not Enough*.

little shock of white feathers on his black head and named him Jon Davidson, after the '70s TV host who had a similar shock of white hair. Jon Davidson (the human) had that blandly handsome look that was popular for men in the '70s. Safe and vacuous. They were the iceberg lettuce of heartthrobs. I had to pretend that Jon having the same name as me meant nothing at all.

Well, I sat in the Penguin House at the Central Park Zoo for hours at a time, over several days that week, determined to wow Lady Buckley with my mimicking skill.

And wow her I did when, after my meditation, I got up in front of the class, stood on a block, took a moment to center myself, and *became* Jon Davidson (the penguin). I fluttered my wings, I shook my head, I pecked at imaginary bugs in my feathers and when I was done, I saw tears in Ms. Buckley's eyes. I assumed the rest of the class was as bored as I had been watching *them*, but she was riveted, smiling proudly at me, tears streaming down both cheeks. I had a moment of thinking: *This bitch is making it about her*—but I quickly dispelled such negative thoughts. It was without a doubt, the best acting I had ever done in my life. Jon Davidson-Penguin was more real than I ever was. The next week, I had to take extra shifts at the restaurant where I waited tables, and didn't have time to study a homeless person, which was the next assignment. I decided to make it all up, but she knew I was faking. And she totally called me on it. Betty was witchy that way.

I've always loved penguins—even before it became fashionable. In 2004, when I heard about the Gay penguins—Roy and Silo—at the Central Park Zoo, I made a special trip from Los Angeles to see them.

The first thing I did was look for Jon Davidson-Penguin, but I couldn't find him anywhere. Maybe he had passed. I didn't know how long penguins live. I wasn't too upset though. I'd gotten what I needed from him anyway, so bye-bye, Jon.

But there were those two tuxedoed queens I had come to see. Roy and Silo. Looking dashing and in love as they took turns sitting on the rock they were proudly trying to hatch. Penguins may be adorable, but they are dumb, dumb, dumb. It really did seem like love to me: the way they groomed each other, entwined their necks, and engaged in what the zookeeper described as an "ecstatic display." Later, I heard they were given a real egg from a female who had abandoned it. Thank god for unfit mothers. Eventually, the egg hatched, and Roy and Silo raised a healthy baby girl named Tango, feeding her regurgitated smelt until she was able to live on her own. It's a love story for the ages.

I spent several hours at the Penguin House that day. And it didn't feel weird. Maybe because I had spent so much time there years earlier, I felt comfortable. And I watched the tourists flow in and ask for the Gay penguins. They would take pictures and smile, but I thought: *Do they really get how important this is? They may think it's cute, but do they think it's* natural*?*

And being New York, there were a few crazies with signs, picketing in front of the zoo. "HOMOSEXUALITY IS A SIN" and "GAY PENGUINS ARE AN ABOMINATION." Although, on that sign the word "Gay" was sort of bent and from a certain angle it appeared to read, "PENGUINS ARE AN ABOMINATION." That made me laugh. The idea of protesting animals you didn't like. Personally, I would protest the ostrich. If God made a mistake, it was there.

And I thought of the book of Genesis, or what I remembered of it from church school. Yes. Church school. No one batted an eye when us Catholic kids were allowed to leave early one day a week and were marched to the "church school" to be bored to death by Sister Clotilda. Yes. Sister Clotilda. *That was her name.* I recall very little from the way she droned on about Genesis—girl was not a compelling speaker—but apparently God threw some sort of cosmic hissy fit and wanted to start over by flooding the planet. And he asked Noah to help him—to build an ark and gather up two of every animal. Male and female, naturally, so they could have lots of unsafe sex and reproduce.

Of course, same-sex couples such as Roy and Silo would not have been welcomed on Noah's Ark. They wouldn't have made it through the first screening. Though, from what I understand about penguins, their genitals are small and hidden, so Noah would have had to look uncomfortably close to find them.

I felt that Roy and Silo had to be nurtured. Treated with care. And I was happy that they were kept somewhere safe.

It's important to find a safe space.

My earliest memory of feeling safe was under a desk in the room I shared with my older brother. I had sawed off the drawers and strung a curtain in front for privacy. I would retreat there after school to do homework and read Hardy Boys books by flashlight until prime time started. I even decorated it with Christmas lights and a picture of Greg Evigan from *B. J. and the*

Bear, ripped from my sister's *Tiger Beat* magazine.[14] It was my own private tabernacle. My sacred space. My personal "church school." But to someone looking in, it probably more closely resembled an eight-year-old's version of a Gay bar.

It was there where I would study my treasured box of Doan's Pills.

I first suspected something was different about me when I fell in love with the man on the box of Doan's Pills. I can still see it today...mainly because I still have it tacked up on a bulletin board in my office at home. The bright red box with a drawing of a man's back on it, the man slightly hunched over, holding his side, obviously in pain. It was so sexy to me.

My mom had back pain and had sought relief from Doan's, but when I discovered it, I stole it from my parent's room. What was her back pain to me when I was confronted with a sexy mystery to solve? Who was this man with the muscly back? Why was he in pain? What did he look like from the front? Was his chest hairy? So many questions, and so much shame to sift through on my way to the answers.

I decided he worked in construction since that seemed like a job where one's back might become sore. I also decided he looked like *Magnum, P.I.*, since I basically wanted *every* man to look like *Magnum, P.I.*[15] He was kind and spent time with his kids. He never raised his voice or hit them, in spite of the fact

14 Greg Evigan was the star of a '70s TV show called *B. J. and the Bear*. (Of course, the Gays got there again with *B. J. From the Bear*.) Note: The "Bear" of the title was a monkey. It is unclear why. *Tiger Beat* was a magazine featuring the sexually nonthreatening boy stars of the day. Gay kids would steal copies from their sister's room when she was at the mall getting her ears pierced and shoplifting root beer flavored lip gloss.

15 We've already talked about Tom Selleck, we don't need to do it anymore. Besides, I don't like what I heard his politics are—though I'm too lazy to Google it.

that he was in constant pain. And he didn't care that I might be different and lived under a desk.

In church school, I liked when we talked about Noah because I pictured him as looking like the man on the box of Doan's Pills. Construction worker's body, similar back pain. I wished Noah had Doan's Pills. And I was convinced he had a hairy chest like *Magnum, P.I.*, since there wasn't as much manscaping back then.

The only person I ever showed my box to was Danny Mortell, a boy a year younger than me who lived up the street and who everyone agreed was even odder than I was. Danny was a strange, wild kid who went barefoot all summer and even into fall. He cut his own hair and, when provoked, would fall on his back and kick wildly at his attackers. "There's something not right about that Mortell kid," my father would say. That's when I knew we had to be friends.

Danny Mortell was also the only one on my block with a pool, which, as far as I was concerned, sealed our bond. It was the shitty above-ground kind, metal and rusty with nails everywhere just waiting for the unsuspecting foot or arm to slice open. It seemed to be made of tetanus and water. Plus, it was missing several boards in the wraparound deck, making it particularly dangerous to play Marco Polo since the person who was "it" had to have their eyes closed when out of the water. I remember one awful time when Scotty Mantor barely got out "Marco!" before disappearing through the hole in the deck.

But my parents never cared about the various injuries because the pool at the Mortell's house got me out of their hair all summer. It may have given us infections, but to us, it was perfect. It was our Penguin House.

Danny and I used to act out the movie *The Poseidon Adventure* in his pool, and, displaying an enviable self-confidence, he always played the girl parts—including Susan, the Pamela Sue Martin role.[16] And I never argued. He had better legs. And when he whipped off his beach towel gown to reveal a cute pair of shorts when his "Susan" had to climb the upside-down Christmas tree to safety, it just seemed to make sense.

I was usually relegated to playing Acres, the slightly femmy steward played by Roddy McDowall. Or Reverend Scott, the hip priest played by Gene Hackman, who tries to lead the survivors to the bottom—now the top—of the capsized ship. There was something about a priest doubting his faith that appealed to me at the time. I would hang from a tree branch over the pool and rail at God the way Gene Hackman did as he tried to shut off a heat valve to make it safe for the others to pass. "What more do you want from us?! We didn't ask you to fight for us, but goddammit, don't fight *against* us! We've come all this way, no thanks to you! How much more blood? How many more liiiiiiives? Belle wasn't enough! Acres wasn't enough! And now the girl!"—It always annoyed me that he didn't mention the Stella Stevens character by name—"You want more blood, you want more lives—then take mine!" At that point, I would fall to my death into the fire (dirty pool water).

Sometimes, one or two of the other weirdos from the neighborhood would join us and take whatever part they were assigned. But we knew to never take on the Shelley Winters role. No,

16 *The Poseidon Adventure* was a '70s movie (remade in 2006 as *Poseidon*). Disaster movies were very big at the time and starred familiar faces from TV and film. The genre began to wane with The Swarm, a film about killer bees. At that time we were terrified of killer—or Africanized—bees, which turned out to be a thinly disguised racist myth.

she belonged to Danny, and when it came time for her death scene, he would drop his Pamela or his Stella or his loopy Carol Lynley and slip easily into his Shelley. No one could touch his Shelley. He was a sight to behold as he morphed into the kindly fat lady who valiantly rescued my Reverend Scott from certain drowning only to suffer a massive coronary upon reaching the surface. His death scene was sublime, and though I wanted desperately to try to take on Shelley myself, I never said a word. I knew I was in the presence of a master and could never come close to his performance. Besides, it was his pool, and Syracuse was just too humid in the summer to risk losing that.

When the weather turned cold, we'd play *The Towering Inferno* in his cluttered basement, his father's pool table filling in nicely for the doomed building. After *The Poseidon Adventure*, it was my favorite disaster movie. I was very affected by it. And by one scene in particular. Jennifer Jones plays a sixty-something teacher of deaf students, leading an honorable but lonely life until she meets Fred Astaire on, as luck would have it, the night the skyscraper catches on fire and the shit hits the fan.

Saintly Jennifer risks her life to save a cat and some deaf kids, one of whom is played by Bobby Brady (Mike Lookinland). This senior citizen is then made to dodge explosions, climb twisted wreckage in an evening gown, and suffer various other ignominies until she is finally rewarded with a much-coveted spot on the scenic elevator with Faye Dunaway and the mayor's hefty wife. This beautiful glass elevator is supposed to deliver all the important women, the two annoying deaf kids and the probably sedated cat to safety on the ground. But just as all seems like it might finally start to go her way, there is another explosion, the elevator tilts, and they toss her ass out. But not before her final selfless act. She's holding the little deaf girl, and in her last moments, knowing she's a goner, she throws the kid into Faye's arms. Then Jennifer, her studio days long behind her, falls backward out of the elevator to her death and my horror. And if that weren't enough, we have to witness her bounce against numerous ledges and balconies on the way down.

I remember thinking: *It's so unfair*. We're made to care for this lovely woman who is so brave and sweet and lonely, and just as she meets someone deserving of her, she winds up as roadkill on the sidewalk. Even hardened fireman Steve McQueen has to turn away. And all Fred Astaire gets is her cat, given to him by O. J. Simpson. Unfair!

But recreated perfectly on Danny's father's pool table, with Danny, of course, as the Jennifer Jones character. He may have been an odd child to most, but he could bring doomed middle-aged women to life like no one I have seen since.

Somewhere in high school, I lost touch with Danny. At that age, you don't want to rock the boat, and he was just too "risky" to have as a friend. Over the years, I would get occasional reports from people. He moved to Rochester. He was go-go dancing in a Gay bar in Buffalo. Then one day, my mother sent me his obituary from the *Syracuse Herald-Journal*. It said he had died after a struggle with leukemia. And later, when I talked to my mother, I knew she didn't believe it either. Her voice got lower when she said, "I don't think it was leukemia."

I sent flowers and a card to his parents. I wrote, "I'm sorry for your loss." I would've liked to have added, "I'm sorry for my loss too," but that didn't seem right somehow.

I wondered if he'd ever found a safe place. Or at least another pool where he could feel safe. I was pretty sure that if he had, it wasn't in Buffalo.

And I decided if there ever was a flood again, I would build an ark. Or at least hire someone to oversee the construction. My ark would be covered in Christmas lights and pictures of hairy-chested '70s TV stars. And it would welcome all the odd animals, the extra ones who don't have a place anywhere else. The single, the old, the sick, the Gay, even the straight ones who are in a relationship but just don't want kids. All the ones that Noah, or whoever his modern equivalent would be, had no room for. Because they deserve a place too. I might even consider the ostrich, even though they freak me out.

We might not be able to repopulate the world by the time the waters recede, but I think we'd have a lot more fun trying.

Eddie Roach And His Fat Finger

When I wasn't huddled under my desk, I could often be found under the slide at the playground where us nerds and maybe-Gays huddled for safety. There was a lot of huddling in a lot of different spaces for kids like us. It was called a playground, but for us it was a mine field in 'Nam. And there was safety in numbers. The thinking was if Kevin Gross, the school bully, found us, he would only have the time and focus to pick off one of us. We would watch that one being dragged away, feeling bad for him but also happy because it wasn't us. Then we would close ranks and tighten the huddle. The slide wasn't perfect cover, but one made do with what one had.

And then one day, Eddie Roach got his finger stuck in one of the holes in one of the steps, and it was the beginning of the end. He had to be *cut* out of it. I remember how much he cried and the flurry of teachers and firemen who ran this way and that. And the sparks that flew in the air as the saw made its way through the metal towards his stupid finger. And I remember hating him because I saw the writing on the wall: The slide would be removed forever. And I was right. Like soldiers in Vietnam, we were forced to leave the protective canopy of trees and march into a field where we were open to enemy fire.

I was directed to my next safe house by something I loathed about myself—my lisp. Cute on Cindy Brady when she was little; not so cute on Susan Olsen, who played her, when spewing homophobic vitriol on the radio as an adult. And definitely not cute on a boy who lived in America in the '70s instead of Spain at any time.

I can't remember whose idea it was to send me to speech therapy. My parents? A teacher? I'd like to think it was someone who had my best interest at heart. But more likely, the thought process was: *Jesus Christ, this kid's gonna grow up a fag unless we do something fast.*

At a certain time every day, I was excused from class and sent away to be de-faggoted. I'm not sure if the other kids knew where I was going. I know they looked envious as I was escorted out. I liked to pretend I was leaving because I was needed somewhere. Maybe a top secret mission. I was to help our country in some vague patriotic way. Probably against the Russians. I mean, we hated them, right? It was their fault we had to have those practice drills where we would hide under our desks in case of nuclear attacks. Even then, I remember thinking: *My skin is going to melt off, but I do like the under the desk thing.*

The speech therapy room was really not a room. It was a converted utility closet that held a small table, three chairs and barely enough room for Mrs. Mapp, me, and Sharon Dumbrowski, who could not for the life of her say her *r*'s correctly. Can there really be a god if a girl with the surname Dumbrowski has a "defect" of some sort?

Every day after lunch, Mrs. Mapp, Sharon "Dumb-Dumb" Dumbrowski, and I would sit in our closet and play Snakes and Ladders, Candy Land, and other classic board games. We were forced to be as verbal as possible in our closet-hour, where "safe" sometimes blurred into "hell." Every time we rolled the dice, Mrs. Mapp made us say our numbers out loud. To this day, I am still triggered by the number six. She would repeat "Teeth together, tongue behind them!" at me so many times that I felt like a Russian orphan being groomed to go undercover in the States until my mission was revealed.

But I have to give her credit—I think it worked. My breakthrough came during a particularly stressful game of Hungry Hungry Hippos. I remember Mrs. Mapp, my Russian handler, standing over me shouting, "What is 'hippo' short for? What is 'hippo' short for?!" until I yelled the answer she was demanding through clenched teeth—tongue behind them. Helen Keller had her "water," I had my "hippopotamus." I hated her and her cat glasses, but I really appreciate her now. It worked. For the most part. I mean, I think I still have a lisp, but I also think most of it's in my mind.

Sadly, the safety of my lisping closet was not going to last forever. A young questioning Gay had to be creative. The darkness of the dollar movie theater. The twisted metal of an old dugout left in the woods behind the Little League fields. And eventually...drama.

Drama. The Gays love drama. And they will go to great lengths to find it. A club devoted to drama? A...drama club, if you will? I'm in! Drama is safe for the Gays. It's basically their Gay bar until they're old enough to move somewhere where their Gay bar is their Gay bar.

And what's that, you say? I can major in drama at college? Yes, please! That will give me a place where I feel I belong *and* will piss off my parents. Where do I sign?

From there, it was just a hop, skip, and a swish to an actual Gay bar—which is drama club with alcohol. The first Gay bar I ever went to was Boy Bar on St. Marks.[17] I had only been in NY for a week or two and was waiting tables at Wylies Restaurant on Fiftieth and First, across from the UN building. We would get dignitaries and ambassadors and occasionally a president of this country or a prime minister of that. We never paid much attention because, whoever they were, all we cared about was not getting them sat in our section. They had diplomatic immunity, and I guess that meant immunity from tipping as well. At the end of one shift, as we sat counting our meager earnings, my fabulous new waitress friend, Gina, asked me what my favorite Gay bar was. When I told her I hadn't been to one yet, she looked aghast. And I think askance at the same time, if that's possible. "We're going out," she declared.

She took me to Boy Bar, and it was like entering Narnia. But with go-go boys. There were rooms full of men who liked men, the occasional woman who liked women, and a handful of straight women—like my fabulous new friend Gina—who liked to drink and dance somewhere other than a straight bar, which always seemed a bit unsafe.

Clubs made me nervous. They were just too big for me. Sure, I had my ecstasy-fueled nights dancing on a floor packed

[17] Boy Bar was a Gay bar on St. Mark's Place, which was a very fun, very Gay street in the East Village. I remember very little of it for chemical reasons, but I distinctly remember making out with the extremely talented drag queen Varla Jean Merman while she was dressed as a Vegas showgirl. And I vaguely recall it being filmed by someone with a camcorder.

with sweaty, sweaty men, like any red-blooded American homo. I can even recall taking off my shirt when the X kicked in and kept my body shame in check.[18] But I would always prefer a good old-fashioned, God-not-fearing Gay bar. They had everything: Newspapers and magazines filled with information you needed and ads for phone sex lines, which you needed even more. And Jukeboxes. And hot bartenders. And people of different ages. And always a friendly drug dealer.

They did not, however, have good bathrooms. I remember many a night praying I wouldn't have to take a coke dump because the toilet stalls were often doorless. Those were the nights you found out who your real friends were. As much as I liked hanging out, I could never stay till closing when the beer goggles went on and it was "take what you can get" time. I got tired. I would usually leave at midnight like Cinderella. But instead of running out gracefully and leaving behind a glass slipper, I would make my way to the door shooting angry looks at the guys who I wouldn't be fucking that night. It was a look that said, "We could get this over with now and get a decent six hours sleep!" It was a look that never worked.

The Pyramid Club on Avenue A became my home away from home. It was not a safe space in the literal sense. I'm pretty sure they only had the one way in and out. Every time I entered, I would think: *Is this the night there is a disaster, and I am trampled to death by drag queens and young Gays rushing to the door, drink tickets still clutched in their hands?* But it was a place where

18 "X" was what we called ecstasy back in the day. It's now more commonly known under various names like MDMA, Molly, or Mandy. Whatever, it made it easier to say "I love you!" to all my friends, even the ones I didn't like, and I support that.

I could write and perform. And, with my friends, find a creative outlet in a profession where you have so little control.

My acting career at this point consisted of the occasional local commercial and many karaoke videos that played on big screens behind the "singer." The lyrics scrolled over the videos, so I guess the audience could join in if the "performer" sucked. They were generally innocuous. I got to be the worshiped boyfriend in "I Say a Little Prayer," the photographer in "Girls on Film," and a '50s era saxophonist in "La Bamba." I didn't think that particular concept really fit the song, and I worried a bit about the racial message it was sending, but I was glad for the fifty bucks. Over the years, I've wondered if I'd ever see any of my videos on a karaoke screen, but I never have. I suspect they were made for the Japanese market, and I'd like to think if I went to Japan, I would be swarmed by fans who recognize me, demanding I host my own Karaoke contest on a reality show.

The comedy group I formed at the Pyramid with my future writing partner, Tracy, and our friends, Diana, Carla, and Hedda Lettuce, and called *Loud Blouse*. We did our thing all over downtown Manhattan, from seedy performance spaces to slightly less seedy performance spaces. We were good! We were very "theatrical."

At the time, the subways were running a public service advertising campaign called *La Decision*. It was basically a bilingual photo-novella promoting condom use. Reading it gave you somewhere to put your eyes at a time when there was no air conditioning on the subway and you wanted to focus on something other than your back sweat as it trickled into your butt crack. And try not to think about that sweaty asshole who was man-spreading, preventing the sweaty pregnant lady from sitting down. No doubt there were several people who wanted to say something to the guy, but Bernhard Goetz was still fresh in all our minds.[19]

La Decision starred Marisol, a pretty, trusting Latina who, in the first episode, tries to get her boyfriend, Julio, to use a condom. He refuses. And as he storms out, Marisol sobs, "I love you, but not enough to die for you!" Such a good exit line, girl.

And such a good idea to parody. Loud Blouses' most in-demand sketch was called "Getting to Know You." And it was told from the point of view of Marisol's vagina, which went on a killing spree, avenging all women who were coerced by men into having unsafe sex. Diana played the vagina, and that was only fitting since the costume she wore was modeled after hers. She was a force in her huge pink and fur costume, biting off Julio's head and then going dancing at the Clit Club—which was a real Lesbian bar in the Meatpacking District. You had to walk through hanging cow carcasses and bloody sidewalks to get to it, but it was worth the stench.

A few years later, when I moved to LA, I had some of my stuff shipped over, including the vagina costume which was in my possession. And, of course, it got lost in the delivery. When asked by the airport official what the contents of that giant box were, I almost told the truth but, in the end, decided to go with a "giant fig" costume. Embarrassment was avoided all around. Sadly, the roof of our garage caved in when El Niño hit in the early '00s and "Vag" was destroyed. I felt terrible. I hadn't protected her from the elements. I hadn't kept her safe.

19 Bernard Goetz was a racist who, in 1984, shot four Black kids on the subway when they allegedly tried to rob him. His actions empowered the NRA to successfully campaign for looser restrictions on carrying concealed firearms. He ran for mayor but lost.

Gay bars are always the first thing I look for when traveling. Depending on the country, there are varying levels of safety for the Gay traveler. One became reliant on the term "Gay-friendly" in pre-Google travel guides. And if there weren't any bars or Gay-friendly spaces noted, a sharp-eyed Gay learned to look for clues to where he might find others like himself. Once, I spotted the tiniest rainbow sticker in the corner of a shop window in Jakarta, Indonesia. When I opened the door and that little bell rang and the owner and I made eye contact, I knew I was home.

Sadly, the Gay bars are disappearing, replaced by dating and hookup apps. What few remain have became Gay/straight bars with bachelorette parties nightly. Or NYU dorms. Or upscale American gastro pubs, whatever those are. I'm saddened by the thought that younger Gays will never remember that very specific smell of balls, beer, poppers, and desperation. And how when you opened that door and smelled that smell, you knew you were safe. Safe to be yourself.

A few years ago, I friended Eddie Roach on Facebook, and the next time I was in Syracuse, we met on the playground of Chestnut Hill Elementary and got high. He couldn't stop laughing when I told him what he took from me. I was aghast and for sure askance. He had done it again—made me feel unsafe on this playground. I walked away angry at him. And at this stupid playground, which had been made "safe" with recycled rubber tire products replacing the cold hard cement.

Where was this shit when Kevin Gross pushed me down every recess?

Save Me, Helen Keller!

As a kid, I had the usual heroes: Batman, Superman, Spiderman, and so on. But my favorite superhero, the one who really inspired me, who I wanted most to be like, was Helen Keller.[20]

This was not something I shared with my friends. When picking which superheroes we would be on the playground, I never said, "I've got dibs on Helen Keller!" And even if I did, I'm not sure how I would have *become* Helen. As Helen, I could not have pretended to fly off the jungle gym or break bricks with my head. And I could not transform myself into her by merely tying a beach towel around my neck like I could the others. Helen was not splashy. Becoming her would be complicated and would seem to involve a bit of cross-dressing and not even in a modern, stylish way. So, I kept my love of her a secret, but I worshipped her nonetheless.

[20] Helen Keller was born in 1880, lost her sight and hearing as a baby, and went on to become a prolific author and activist. Where's the Barbie version of her?

She was my hero. But not for the usual Helen Keller reasons, such as how she overcame extreme diversity or how she helped prove that people with disabilities offer so much to society. I loved her because she received so much sympathy from people.

In his book Barrel Fever, David Sedaris wrote, "If you're looking for sympathy you'll find it between shit and syphilis in the dictionary." As much as I love David Sedaris, I cannot agree with his feelings on this subject. Sympathy was all I ever wanted as a child. And besides you'll also find the word sympathy between shortcake and syrup. Sweet!

At a very early age, I knew I was different. But I also knew it wasn't a *good* different. Of course, it wasn't as bad as my girl Helen's. (Though I envied her for being allowed to run around the dinner table eating off everyone's plate with impunity). I knew I was unlikely to become a hero like her. There was never going to be a kid on a playground with a beach towel tied around his neck yelling "I'm Batman!" as another kid runs behind him, latte in hand and wrinkle cream on his eyes, screaming "I'm Jon!"

So, I figured out the way to survive was to get people to feel sorry for me. I needed their pity. And I knew how I was going to get it.

I had it all planned out. I would meet the woman who was to be the love of my life when I entered my mid-to-late teens. Much like Kristy McNichol did in *Summer of My German Soldier.*[21] Only in my version, I was Kristy and my lover was not a Hitler Youth. But, like that star-crossed couple, our love was forbidden because she was beautiful. And Black. I realize

[21] Kristy McNichol was a YA star of TV and film with a boyish charm, kind of a low rent Jodie Foster. Check out *Little Darlings* with her and Tatum O'Neal—it's pretty great, but probably terrible.

now there were aspects to this fantasy designed just to piss off my parents.

We would have a child, a little girl—sometimes they were boy and girl twins—and be deliriously happy for a short period of time until she was killed in a fiery car accident. I would come home from work to find the police at my door and neighbors with pity in their eyes, the women wringing their aprons (aprons were often wrung in my fantasies). My wife had been made unalive. It was tragic. And I was forced to raise my kid—or kids—alone. In this fantasy, I would be devastated and would never recover. Certainly, I would never date again. People would say, "What about this girl or that girl? Why don't you go out with her?" And I'd say, "No. I had my one true love, and now I'm done." I would feel their sad eyes on me as I walked bravely away toward my little girl slash little twins who looked so much like my late, lamented wife. I would be a widower. And I would be free. It was perfect. Then I wouldn't have to deal with messy, messy feelings such as: *Why does Mark Spitz make my painter's pants tight?*[22]

As time went on, this fantasy became more and more elaborate. Sometimes I found a clue that my wife might still be alive, and I'd spend the rest of my life traveling the highways and byways of America in a funky van looking for her. Or sometimes, in a version that even confused me, I was forced to put my grief on hold because my country needed me to go

22 Mark Spitz was a multi gold medal–winning Olympic swimmer. When he stepped up to the platform in his speedo and mustache, America got a boner. Then we were edged for decades, until Ricky Martin danced and sang "La Copa de la Vida" at the World Cup Final in 1998 and we finally shot our collective wad.

to the Middle East and kill an evil prince whose boyfriend I remarkably resembled. I had dumped the kids at this point.

Eventually, as I entered my teens, I became more practical, more realistic in my search for sympathy. And I feared it wouldn't come from something beautiful like the death of a fictional beard.[23]

I became convinced that I would lose one of my senses. Most likely my sense of sight or hearing. Those were really the only two I spent time worrying about. I could envision a car accident where I hit my head so hard I lost my hearing. Or a brain tumor would slowly and dramatically rob me of my eyesight like Bette Davis in *Dark Victory*.[24] But I had difficulty envisioning an accident or an illness that suddenly robbed me of my sense of taste. That wouldn't get much sympathy from people. However, the thought that it would probably stop the stress eating and take my jeans from husky to petite, did give me pause.

No, if I was going to lose a sense, it was going to be my sight or my hearing. But losing my sight seemed horrible. To never see a movie or a TV show again? I couldn't bear that. It seemed a fate worse than death. I was just a kid, and my personality at this point didn't really exist. It was just some weird mixture of things cannibalized from the people I observed on TV, in the movies, or in the cheesy paperbacks I read nonstop. If my eyes were suddenly taken away from me, who would I be? Just some pimply, unformed mix of Jack Tripper from *Three's*

---

23 A beard was a girl or woman who was (or was perceived to be) the girlfriend or wife of a closeted boy or man. Her awareness of this was nice but, sadly, not required.

24 Dark Victory is a sappy movie from 1939. Socialite Bette Davis lives a lavish but emotionally empty life, until she is humbled by losing her sight to a brain tumor. She's bummed she can't ride horses anymore. But there's a happy ending because stable man Humphry Bogart likes her better blind.

Company, The Bionic Woman, and the Trans ex-football player from *The World According to Garp.*[25]

Besides, I saw firsthand what being blind did to you when my friend, Bernadette Rossi, came back from summer vacation wearing a scarf to cover her head—which was bald from radiation treatments—and eyes that no longer saw because of a brain tumor. The previous year, we had met and become fast friends. She was overweight and unpopular, and I was Gay and unpopular. It was a match made in Hag Heaven. And in Fag Heaven, if I'm to be equally offensive—which is something we never were back in the day. Progress![26]

She made me laugh, and I remember thinking: *Maybe this girl is the one. That perfect girlfriend every young boy like me is looking for. The girl who would protect me from ridicule and never ask to be kissed. And maybe one day, God willing, have my twins and then die in some TBD way, while still looking beautiful.*

It would have been perfect, but then she had to come back blind. And when she finally showed up again at school, the moment came for me to say hello as she uncertainly tapped her way down the hall towards me. But I didn't. I didn't say anything. I just held my breath, stepped out of the way, and let her go on. I didn't know what to say to her, wasn't sure how to

25 *Three's Company* was a groundbreaking sitcom that brought Gays and straights togther to laugh at Gays. *Bionic Woman* was a spin-off of *The Six Million Dollar Man,* both of which I loved, both of which have been remade. I think. Computer will know. *The World According to Garp* must be read right after this book. Though I suspect the Trans character, Roberta, doesn't get the most informed treatment, she was my first introduction to a Trans woman and we all fell in love with her.

26 "Hag" (a shortened version of "fag hag," though equally offensive) was a derogatory word used for the female friend of a Gay man. It fell out of favor when we all realized it was a horrible way to refer to a friend. Though I'm told Elizabeth Taylor, the OG hag, wore it as a badge of honor.

be friends with a blind person. But mostly I wasn't sure how I felt. I was both envious of all the attention she was getting and relieved it wasn't me. I felt like I'd dodged a bullet somehow.

No, deaf would be the way I'd have to go, though it would sadden me to not be able to play records on my Close 'n Play record player anymore. Well, I suppose I could still *play* my 45s, but I would be unable to hear Cher sing "Mama (When My Dollies Have Babies)" from her album, *With Love, Chér*—she briefly played with an accent in her name—and I would sorely miss that.

Besides, I'd always been fascinated by the idea of deafness. Sure, one of the happiest days of my childhood was the day my doctor told my mother that my headaches were because I needed glasses, but Bernadette had soured me on blindness. And anyway, hadn't blind been done to death? I mean, it seemed like something *anyone* could do. From Stevie Wonder to Melissa Sue Anderson on *Little House on the Prairie*.[27] It didn't seem special anymore. At least Helen Keller had the good sense to lose more than one sense.

When I was a junior in high school, a mixed-race deaf kid was discovered in town and quickly enrolled at Liverpool High, where I went. I mean discovered literally. I no longer remember the exact details, but who cares? Basically, Randy was found in a closet, where he had lived his entire life. Apparently, his parents thought he was "*r********"[28] and that he would be fine in a closet, only to be mortified later when they learned he wasn't at all what the *r* word connoted, but in fact, deaf. And, as was

27 Ugh, another '70s TV show. I watched a lot of TV as a kid. But it paid off!

28 A word we thought was okay to use back in the day, often as a slur or to get a laugh. It was briefly revived—to much derision—in that movie with Robert Downey Jr. that I've forgotten the name of.

also soon discovered, a really fast runner. I can only think that growing up in a closet might tend to make one want to run a lot and run fast. Anyway, a big deal was made of him, and a few high schools argued that, despite the fact that he didn't live in their district, he should attend their school. Each claimed they could best serve his needs, but secretly, each wanted a track star. He became a mini-celebrity in town, eclipsing even the fifteen-year-old girl who gave birth to twins in her room without anyone knowing she was even pregnant and then throwing only one of them away in the garbage at the curb. And it worked in his favor that he was superhot. "He's very handsome," people would say, and then add in a whisper "It's not his fault he's m******, poor thing."[29]

They say losing a sense makes your other senses heightened, and it's true. To me, his sense of hotness increased tenfold. His smile could lift a car off a baby.

And I was so jealous. He possessed the two things I longed for, the only two things that mattered: sympathy and good looks. He was perfect. I loved him, hated him, and was determined to make him mine. We had so much in common, I reasoned. We both knew what it was like to live in a closet.

He fascinated me, and I spent most of my senior year trying to become his friend. But it wasn't easy. He was very guarded, and I understood that. I guess it would be hard to develop people skills when for most of your life all your friends were hangers.

I finally got my chance at the prom. I was delighted to be seated at the same table with him and his date, a mousy, unpopular girl with cotton candy hair who only got the honor

[29] Another derogatory word that died out but has undoubtedly made a comeback in parts of the South, if it ever really went away at all.

of going with him because she knew sign language for some reason. My date, however, was not very pleased with the seating arrangement. Even though we had the deaf guy, we were not the most popular table and her time in this country was running out. Soon she would have to return to Liverpool, England, which had a foreign exchange program with Liverpool, New York. (Apparently, they are "sister cities," but I've been to both, and they are the sisters who were never once asked to dance and now live in their own filth in matching trailers on opposite sides of the Atlantic.)

Her name was Missy Bell, and she made it clear when she asked me that I was her fourth or fifth choice. But I didn't care. I just wanted to be anywhere Randy was. Any fears that Missy might expect something sexually after the prom were allayed when she went to talk to friends and basically didn't return.

I never picked up the official prom photos of Missy and I from her host family, but I rushed directly to the Fotomat and had my personal pictures developed, which consisted almost entirely of my hot deaf runner by himself and then paired with others when he began to get suspicious.[30] I was such a good friend to him that night. "Hi, Wes! Let me get a picture of you with Randy." "Sharon, hi! You look nice—let me get a picture of you with Randy." "Now Randy, alone. Smile, Randy!"

I stared. *A lot.* I knew I shouldn't, but I couldn't stop myself. This didn't go unnoticed by Randy. There were many moments of me quickly looking away when he tried to catch me at it.

[30] Fotomat was a franchise of kiosks that stood in parking lots. Basically, you drove up, dropped your film off, came back the next day, and it was ready. It felt like the future! But if the photos were untoward or Gay, you wouldn't get them back. But at least you felt good knowing some perv was jerking off to your pix in the bathroom at the photo developing place.

I must've looked like an idiot whipping my head around and pretending to stare at something on the wall or on my hand as if it were the most interesting thing in the world.

I didn't know! I didn't know how to act! Was I giving out signals? Was I supposed to? And did I even want to? Why wasn't there someone to talk to without risk? Someone safe? Or anonymous? Like a confessional booth, but where a boy who thinks he likes another boy might get information? Un-hateful information. Maybe be sent away with a pamphlet, *So You're Having Same-Sex Feelings—Let's Rap About That!* Maybe the typical "ten Hail Marys" the priests always asked you to say would become a quiz called "Hail Mary!" and you would have to name ten famous Marys that are icons in the Gay community. Like, Mary Tyler Moore...Mary Poppins...Mary Todd Lincoln (because she was First Hag for a bit). That would be where I would throw the pamphlet out, frustrated I couldn't come up with any more.

There was no road map.

Admittedly, navigating the intricacies of dating is confusing for any teen, but at least straight ones could go to the library and check out the book, *Boys Are So Weird! A Guide for Talking to the Opposite Sex*. Which I did. And by "check out," I mean stole.

> Chapter 9: Saying "I LIKE YOU."
>
> GREG: I had a good time tonight.
>
> JENNY: Me too. (smiles at him hopefully)
>
> GREG: Maybe I'll see you at the game tomorrow?
>
> JENNY: Sure, that sounds nice. (looks down at her feet)

GREG: (looks up at the sky) Well, um…

JENNY: Yes? (smiles softly)

GREG: Um… Goodnight. (kisses her gently)

JENNY: Goodnight. (disappointed)

The book gives the advice to not pressure a boy to say he likes you. Boys have a hard time doing that, and they might get spooked if you push them out of their comfort zone. He will say it in other ways, such as "Flowers or a unique, funny little gift. Or a cute card!"

I imagined the exchange I would have with Randy:

JON: I had a good time at the prom.

RANDY: (signs) It was okay. (starts to walk away)

JON: (stopping him) Maybe I'll see you at the game tomorrow?

RANDY: (signs) Um, let go of my arm, dude. And were you stalking me at the prom? What are you, some kind of psycho fag?

JON: (smiles) Great! Should I pick you up at your house?

RANDY: (creeped out, walks away)

JON: Um…see you tomorrow! (walks down the hall, smiling and thinking about how weird boys are and wondering what unique, funny little gift to get Randy, as every student in the school, and several teachers, laugh at him)

Post prom, I was sure people were talking about what a joke I'd made of myself. I had gone too far, had raised eyebrows and suspicions. I hated myself for letting my guard down and I vowed never to do it again. I wouldn't be seen as different. I would be seen as normal! I probably even told an AIDS joke or two, "What does 'Gay' stand for? 'Got AIDS yet?'" Or "What's the hardest thing about having AIDS? Convincing your parents you're Haitian." Those were popular ones at the time. Randy had come out of his closet forever, but I took a step further into mine, parting the hangers and slipping through the clothes to stand at the very back with the never-used hockey stick.

I spent the summer after graduation working at Fort Ontario in Oswego, New York, as a tour guide. I was assigned to the living quarters and left alone with the "frontier family," which consisted of four mannequins with missing hands bought from a Woolworths and dressed in suede fringe coats and coonskin caps. In two months, I don't think one visitor came, so I spent my time trying to learn sign language from a book in the hope that I would run into Randy somewhere. I never did see him again, however, and that's fine because the only thing I learned to sign was "nice shoes."

Not long ago, Chris and I needed a handyman, and we hired a deaf Gay handyman from the Gay Yellow Pages—which were, of course, known as the Pink Pages.[31] We thought it would be good to give our business to someone with a disability. (And possibly pay off some karmic debt that I owed for being such an asshole to Bernadette.)

He arrived with a gaggle—or giggle, if you will—of Gay cronies to work for him. They were all deaf, and instead of signing *to* each other, they seemed to sign *at* each other, their wrists flailing this way and that like their arms were connected by springs. I think they actually lisped in sign language, which looked more like voguing on them. It was beautiful. As far as being a handyman, Rob sucked. But we didn't fire him because that would prove we weren't good people. And he knew this. And I knew he knew, and he knew I knew he knew, and he didn't care. It worked for him.

In the early '90s I ran into Bernadette, my blind former friend from middle school. I was home in Syracuse for a visit with my family and I saw her in the parking lot of a grocery store where I had worked many years earlier. (I briefly managed the dairy department at Nichols IGA in high school until I got

---

31 The Yellow Pages were part of the phone book—a huge book of the phone numbers and addresses of everyone in town. It was delivered to your house every year for free. They were also put in phone booths. They have mostly gone extinct because they were no longer profitable and kind of dangerous and also because now anyone can find out anything they want about you anyway. A psycho can still find your address, but at least less trees are destroyed. Now, a phone booth was an enclosed metal and glass booth on the street that had a door you could close to make phone calls. You held the phone far from your mouth and ear because a lot of other people didn't. Now, they are either gone or repurposed or left without a purpose at all. Sad. Though, recently I discovered they are still in use in Edinburgh, Scotland, and probably other places in the UK and beyond. Who knew? Fun fact: In the '90s in New York, there was a rumor that someone was putting needles in the change return part. There was also a rumor that someone was spraying water with feces in it over the salad bars at those big delis. Sadly, that one was true.

fired for stealing milk crates to keep my albums in. In fact, it was my mother's idea. "Those would be perfect for your records," she said. "Mom, they're not going to let me just take one." "Then steal it," was her suggestion. She had parked her Nova around back and had the trunk open when I got caught by the owner as I exited the loading dock, a milk crate in each hand.)

Now, it's years later, and I still felt the shame as I exited the store with my power bar and Fiji water to see Bernadette tapping her way towards me. Well, of course, my instinct was to run away, but I reconsidered. *This is a gift*, I decided, and I fully intended to make the most of it. As she got near, I stopped her and told her who I was and she remembered. I told her how much she made me laugh that one year and how it was so nice to have someone to talk to who didn't make fun of me because my voice was all over the place. And then I apologized for ignoring her the next year when she went blind. And she understood. I suggested we go for coffee and catch up. Maybe laugh at the foibles of youth. She hesitated a moment, and then said, "No, thanks." She had to be somewhere. But I knew she was just blowing me off. And she knew that I knew it. And I knew that she knew that I knew It. She was basically telling me that I was an asshole. But I could sense that, under her disdain, she actually felt a bit sorry for me. It was a win for both of us!

Fierce Pussy Plaza

One night several years ago, when I was in Syracuse to visit my parents, I got out of bed to use the bathroom and found my mother in front of the refrigerator looking over her collection of magnets. She had many of them. So many they covered the entire front and spilled onto both sides, though one side was really too close to the wall to see the magnets that stuck there. "I put the dumb ones there," she explained to me once. I guess she considered the acorn with the caption "THE MIGHTY OAK WAS ONCE A NUT LIKE YOU!" worthy of front status.

I started her on this collecting binge when, at eighteen, I went backpacking through Europe for two months and discovered that magnets make great souvenirs. They are small, cheap, and can be bought anywhere—most importantly at airports in a panic just before one gets on a plane home.

As we looked over her collection, I saw the first ones I had bought her, now a little sad and dingy looking. Refrigerator magnets don't age well. There was a beer stein from Germany (the plastic "foam" cracked and dirty), a red telephone booth from England, a tiny loaf of French bread from Paris and, weirdly, a diner-type coffee cup with a dog and cat embracing on it that said "HUGS SERVED HERE," from Yugoslavia, which is now known as Serbia and Montenegro. Probably because Yugoslavia couldn't seem to figure out its brand. These are the first magnets, so they started at the top left corner of the refrigerator and proceeded from there. A map of all my travels over the years. Travels that my mom never quite understood.

"Why do you want to go to Europe?" she asked me after I graduated from high school. It was a pointless question since my friend Glen and I were saying our goodbyes as we were leaving for the airport. We were standing on the lawn of our little black house on Pleasantview Drive. Although whenever I told someone that we lived in a black house, my mother would correct me, "It's *charcoal*." "Charcoal *is* black," I would counter. "Our house is black. *Black*, Mother." I instinctively knew this detail would be important to a shrink one day.

"Why not see *this* country?" she would ask. "They say Lake George is beautiful. It's safe. And they speak English there." But I was determined to go. I had been saving for this trip, and Glen and I were nervous but excited. We knew it would change our lives but were not sure exactly how.

"It's good that he goes, Eleanor," our handsome Italian neighbor, Mario, said to my mom. "He will come back as a man." And this scared me even more because I wasn't sure what he meant, but I suspected it had something to do with vaginas. Mario gave me a look as if to say, "I envy you—the tail you're going to get." We were, I believe, having an *uomo a uomo* moment. I tried to return the smirk, thinking: *If you only knew how often I masturbated to you, Mr. Agostinelli, you would not be smiling conspiratorially at me.*

Tail, however, *was* on my list of worries. Directly above: Do they sell Oxy 10 in Europe?[32] I was convinced that I would have sex with a girl on this trip. It would be easier, I reasoned, since sex happens more often there. The women know what they're doing and will do most of the work. I'm not sure where I got those dubious facts, but they appealed to me. And once and for all, I could finally put to bed those pesky thoughts that I might be Gay just because I wanted to kiss the hairy Italian Grizzly Adams–type next door. [33] I would, indeed, come back an oumo.

I was seventeen, and my experience with girls consisted of some clumsy fumblings and the occasional marathon make out session. Anything beyond that amounted to dirty passages in the paperbacks I tore through, particularly a passage in *Jaws* on page 151, that I still remember to this day. (I had read the novel before the movie came out). Sheriff Brody's wife, Ellen, is imagining an affair with shark expert Hooper, played in the movie by Richard Dreyfuss, but in my mind by *Buck Rogers*'s Gil Gerard.[34] Mrs. Brody, played in the movie by Lorraine Gary—but also in my mind played by Gil Gerard—fantasizes about having sex with Hooper while they are speeding down

[32] OXY 10 was (and maybe still is?) a zit cream. It dried your face out when you slathered it on, but it was liquid gold to me. Do they still make it? How would I know?

[33] Grizzly Adams was another TV hunk from the '70s who brought Gay bear realness into the living rooms of America. Played by Dan Haggerty, Grizzly was a masc, humpy, hairy, sensitive mountain man. Everyone, regardless of gender or orientation, wanted to be held and gently rocked by him. Interesting fact: male body hair seemed to go out of style with the '80s and the onset of AIDS. A connection? Perhaps…

[34] Gil Gerard was yet *another* hot man in a '70s TV show and an integral part of my youth. I remember him filling out his leather pants very nicely. But upon a rewatch as an adult, he seemed a little doughy and the pants did his package no favors. I guess we weren't as picky back then. Fun fact: I'm not as picky now.

the highway, and they are so distracted they crash and are both killed instantly. She giggles as she pictures herself dead on the side of the road, her dress bunched up around her waist and "her vagina yawning open, glistening wet, for the world to see." I must have read that passage a thousand times, committing it to memory, trying hard to picture it. Why exactly was it yawning? Was it tired? Why was it still alive when the rest of Mrs. Brody was not? Whatever the answers were, her vagina definitely knew something I didn't.

The drinking age in Syracuse went from eighteen to twenty-one on the day after my eighteenth birthday, giving me exactly until midnight on December third to get into a bar legally. To celebrate this auspicious event, I had a date with a girl named Stacy Levine. Poor Stacy. I didn't really want to go out with her, though I did like her. She was funny and cute. I just didn't know what I was supposed to do. And this terrified me. In fact, I never would have agreed to a date if she hadn't cornered me and asked. It was weird—the patriarchy seemed to be completely ignored by some girls. I would have been content to hang out, maybe roller-skate or listen to The Go-Go's on my outdated Close 'n Play, but these girls were never satisfied with that for long.

"I really like him," I could hear her saying to her friends, "but I don't know if he likes me." "Tell him," they would counsel. "Guys are dumb. You have to make the first move." Well guys can be dumb, Stacy, but some guys can also be fags.

And then those girls might ask those boys out. And there might be some kissing and maybe something more, but it never ends well. At least not for me and Stacy Levine. I picked her up in my sister's shit-brown Impala, slipping and skidding over the icy December streets of Syracuse. When I pulled the heavy land-boat into Stacy's driveway—which was on a down sloping hill—the car wouldn't stop and rolled until it hit their garage door. After what seemed like an eternity, no one came out to look, and I realized they hadn't heard anything. I broke a large bag of Doritos behind the front wheels for traction, backed up into the street, and honked.

Unsurprisingly, the date was a disaster. Because of the law change, no bar would admit me, even with my desperate plea of "But I have until midnight when the law goes into effect! Then I'll leave! I promise!" My *oumo a oumo* looks over Stacy's head meant nothing to the doormen. We ended up parked behind a Kentucky Fried Chicken, where we made out for hours until she got bored and yawned, which made me think of Sheriff Brody's wife's vagina and the confusion that came with it. Goodbye to you, Stacy Levine and your yawning stuff.

But I understood my mother's fears concerning my Europe trip. My parents had never been farther south than Pennsylvania or farther north than Niagara Falls (the ugly American side). The farthest the family had been was a car trip to Corning, New York, to view the damage from the flood caused by tropical storm Agnes.

I was excited to see the damage, of course, but also to visit the Corningware glass factory where, after the tour, you were allowed to pick one piece of free unbreakable Corningware. I was beside myself and took a good ten minutes before deciding I wanted the butter dish. So white and unblemished and ready for butter. But not so unbreakable, as I found out in the parking lot when my older brother, Jeff, grabbed it from me and smashed it to pieces. "False advertising," he said.

Mine wasn't a family that believed in travel. We only took one real vacation together and that was to Polliwog Pond in northern New York, where my great aunt Tess had a cabin. My father and brother were going fishing, and my sister was going to collect pine cones, so I pretended to be torn—though no one was really surprised when I stayed behind for the activity that didn't involve blood and scales and worms.

Jackie found a bottle and filled it with bits of wildflowers and pretty stones. Not to be outdone, I found a dirty Coke can and filled mine with similar things and we both presented them to my mother.

"Which one do you like better?" I demanded.

"I like them both," was her democratic reply.

But I wasn't happy with that. "No, really. Which one do you like better?"

"I said I like them both."

"Which one, Mother? Pick one."

"Okay, I like this one! I like Jackie's! Jesus Christ, why do you make me do stuff like that?!"

I was devastated but determined she wouldn't see it, so I ran into the woods and threw the can as far as I could. Later in bed, racked with guilt about littering, I went back with a flashlight, emptied the can, and threw it in the trash. We didn't recycle then, so I didn't yet need to feel guilty about that.

Traveling with your family never made much sense to me. One traveled to get *away* from one's family.

During my two months in Europe, I did not have sex. But I did have my pocket picked in a McDonald's in Paris, grow a beard, and have my first real emergency. Glen and I had hooked up with a group of people on the ferry from Brindisi, Italy, to Greece and had stopped in Crete to rent minibikes and tool around the island. Then disaster struck as one of our new friends, Becky, who was from South Africa, rode off a cliff and crashed on the rocks below, sending me into the kitchen of the nearest restaurant screaming, "I need an ambulance! Am! Bu! Lance! Doesn't anyone speak English?!" My mother was right. This would never have happened in Lake George.

Becky had broken her leg in several places but was determined to continue her travels with her hot boyfriend, Leslie, who was from Zimbabwe and very, very racist. but I didn't care about that because he liked me. And he was so handsome. While Glen was understandably upset, I let my horniness win over my outrage. He thought I was cool. No one had ever thought that before.

Maybe that's why you travel: to go to a place where you are not known and can be mistaken for cool.

It turned out my neighbor Mario wasn't exactly right. I don't know if I came home from Europe "a man," but I definitely came home more than halfway to homo and in love with a racist guy from Zimbabwe named Leslie. I felt similar to the way Hooper made Sheriff Brody's wife feel on page 137: "...more intensely feminine than she had in years—a warm, wet feeling both delicious and uncomfortable."

It was a confusing time. Made even more so by his numerous four AM phone calls and eventual visit. It was a little humiliating when he flew across the world to visit me. He was from Africa, somewhere wild and exotic. All I could promise him in Syracuse was a visit to the Salt Museum and some arcade action at "Slots of Fun!" at the mall. My heart was broken when he eventually confided in me that he had flown to the US to escape a charge of negligent homicide in the death of his new girlfriend's child and not so much to be my first boyfriend. But I recovered quickly. After all, he was awful and insane and a murderer. And after he moved on, it amused me to think that my parents had a racist, bisexual, homicidal maniac on the run, sleeping on their couch for a week.

By now, my mother's refrigerator had grown to include random magnets she purchased around town mixed in with the ones I bought her. There were various clowns and kittens and a tiny bathroom scale with the words "I'LL START MY DIET TOMORROW!" on it. Next to that, a plastic pack of cigarettes that, when pushed, emitted a horrible hacking sound that seemed to last an eternity. And at the end of the line was a creepy bear in a wedding dress that she got at an Indian casino. (Are they still called that?) It was time to bring it back to me.

Ironically, I think I came closer to "becoming a man" at Camp Sister Spirit, a Lesbian retreat outside Laurel, Mississippi, that I visited while on a tour of the South with friends. After their failed marriages, two women had fallen in love and decided to open a safe place for Lesbians to commune, craft, do political shit, and fuck around. My friends and I had seen them on *Donahue* talking about the constant harassment from the locals and decided they needed us. We arrived at a parade—which (understandably) was not for us but to celebrate Parker Posey Day. Parker was apparently a local girl made good.

While at Camp Sister Spirit, Heidi and Dana seemed to relax a lot while Tom and I worked like dogs. But I didn't care. I wore white overalls and learned how to use a chainsaw, build a chicken coop, and choke down banana and mayonnaise sandwiches. Even the continual harassment from the locals eventually became fun. We laughed as we were chased out of the hardware store while trying to buy paint to cover the word "faggots" that mysteriously appeared on the front gate every morning. Apparently, they didn't know the word "dyke." We found that almost charming. They celebrated Parker Posey Day, but "dyke" hadn't yet made it to Laurel, Mississippi.

That trip resulted in a magnet of a beaver chewing down a tree.

My mom eventually grew to love the fact that I traveled. The more places I went, the more magnets she would get, and the longer she could look over them and remember.

These days, I find myself traveling to my parents instead of away from them. The little black house on Pleasantview Drive now has tan aluminum siding that I hate. And I think my mother would hate it too. She went into a nursing home a few years ago, and when I flew back to help, the first thing I noticed was the naked refrigerator. My dad had taken off all my mother's magnets and put them in a box. He was going to throw them away, but I stopped him. I don't think he understood their importance. And I'm not sure my mother does now either, but I put a few of her favorites up on her headboard at the nursing home, just in case, including a carrot with googly eyes and the caption "IF FRIENDS WERE CARROTS, I'D PICK YOU." The rest I brought home but could not put up. We have one of those stainless-steel refrigerators that magnets don't stick to, which is just as well since Chris made it very clear he wouldn't have those hideous things in his kitchen anyway.

But two of them I keep on my bedside lamp. One reminds me of my mother. It reads, "WARNING: THESE PREMISES ARE PROTECTED BY KILLER DUST BALLS."

The other is an old homemade magnet of me kissing my late boyfriend, Luis, at a Gay Pride parade under a doctored street sign in the Village that reads: "FIERCE PUSSY PLAZA."

She kept that one on the front near the bottom. I keep it because it reminds me of when I finally felt “man enough” to tell her who I was.

Of Course I Know Tina Turner!

Growing up, I often felt like a foreign exchange student in my family's house. Someone from the far away country of Europe. And they didn't understand me or my strange, unfamiliar ways. They would just let me do my thing, watch from a distance, shake their heads and say, "Who are we to judge? Maybe that's normal where he comes from." This fantasy worked for me. It was a way of dealing with my outsider feelings. It made me feel special and exotic. I think I even once tried a beret.

It wasn't until I got to SUNY Oswego that I realized I could seriously reinvent myself. These were people who literally didn't know me! They would be from far away locales such as New Jersey and Long Island.

At home, I was a closeted geek from Syracuse with little to no self-esteem. At college, I could actually *be* someone from another country! Someone who smoked clove cigarettes and wore scarves indoors and was of indeterminate sexual orientation (I'd heard people in those other counties didn't always decide right away whether they liked boys or girls). And I knew I could pull it off. Years of pretending I was interested in girls and baseball and spitting had made me such a convincing liar, I was sure *this time* I could make that beret work.

As with everything, alcohol helped my plan immensely. Over cheap beers and cheap pot in my dorm room at Oswego State, I informed my new floor mates that I was born in South Africa. That my name was really pronounced "Yon." That I was found in an orphanage and adopted by the Kinnallys of Syracuse. And that I wasn't even really sure how old I was.

And it worked. My successful lies got me a few "cools" from my new druggie friends, the suspicion of the one real foreign student on our floor—Farris, from Jordan—and the attention of a stoner girl from a dorm across campus named Kelly.

Kelly was tough. And fun. She was from Roslyn, New York, and a few years older than me. Alcohol made us instant friends, but our love of Tina Turner cemented things. Kelly liked me, which is not something we necessarily had in common, but it was something I could work with. She thought I was interesting. She had never met anyone from South Africa before. I was an exotic fruit to her.

She insisted we join the apartheid protest on the quad that was coming up—surely coming from South Africa, I wouldn't want to miss that! So I reluctantly gave up a Friday happy hour to stand in a large circle, singing the chorus of "We Are the World" over and over until someone finally had the nerve to break the circle and put an end to our suffering.[35] I don't know if it was the number of students who had also given up their happy hours to unite in a common goal or the strength we felt as we held hands (Kelly holding my right and gazing at me, the hot president of the Social Justice Forum holding my left, me gazing at him), but the meaning of those powerful words sung by Huey Lewis and Diana Ross actually got through to me. I felt empowered. I was the world.

The anti-apartheid demo went so well, there was talk of organizing a trip to Albany to meet with officials about the proposed tuition hike. Kelly wanted to go, and she was sure that, as a man of the world, I would too.

And I did. I wanted to change the world. And more importantly, I wanted to protest the recent change in the drinking age. The second one in as many years—why couldn't this goddamn state let me drink? A future at college separated from alcohol seemed like no future at all. It would be my own private apartheid.

As we were about to sign up for the bus to the event, we learned that Tina Turner was playing at Saratoga Performing Arts Center on the same night, and it wasn't very far from Albany. And I had a great idea.

I suggested that instead of taking the bus, Kelly and I could drive to Albany in her car, be all political and shit, and then go see Tina Turner. Kelly was hesitant. She wasn't supposed to drive her car that far. So I was forced to use my powers of persuasion—meaning I was happy to lie to get my way. I told her I

[35] "We Are the World" was a charity single recorded by the Supergroup USA for Africa in 1985. It was huge. And pretty terrible. But noteworthy because where else would one see Bob Dylan and La Toya Jackson singing together?

actually knew Tina a little and could probably get us backstage to meet her.

I had read somewhere that a believable lie contains a lot of detail. So…I had met Tina at a party in New York. She liked my coat, so I impulsively gave it to her. I said something that amused her, and then she asked JFK Jr. to move over so I could sit down in the booth next to her. She bought me drinks and I made her laugh for *hours.*

I was amazed at how naturally and quickly these lies flowed out of me. It was like second nature. Back then, Gays learned to lie at a very early age to protect themselves, probably as early as babies. I'm sure I laid in that crib, stared at that mobile, and thought: *I've got to make sure there's not a hint of swish in those first steps I'm going to make tomorrow. And I'll force myself to veer toward that stupid truck that Uncle Bad Breath bought me—that'll throw those assholes off the scent.* I think I was a mean baby.

But now, it seemed I was playing on a whole other level, and had gone way past the amateur, standard Gay lies that young men tell young women: "Yes, I have a girlfriend, but she goes to another school." Which, if people got too nosey, could be added to: "…in Canada." Or: "I'm sorry I can't go to your parents' camp with you, I'm having my tonsils out" (not easy to disprove). Or: "Oh my god, I was so drunk, I really couldn't even feel you trying to wake me up for sex" (thank god for college binge drinking). The lies came fast and sounded sincere. It was the Gay superpower.

The meeting in Albany was with some low-level politico who made little to no impression on me. I do remember that we were outraged about the tuition hike and then outraged again by the rising drinking age. At least, Kelly and I were. And my argument basically boiled down to something like: "We can fight for our country, but we can't drink till we puke?!" Powerful stuff, which I'm sure gave that government official pause or whatever. Flush from our political "victory," Kelly and I said goodbye to our annoyed cohorts and headed to the concert in her rusty Datsun.

Don Henley from the Eagles was opening for Tina, but we didn't give a shit. We were too cool for Don Henley. We are in college now. We listened to bands like Suicidal Tendencies and the Butthole Surfers. We went slam dancing. We took acid and smoked skunk weed.

To be honest—which is not something I knew a lot about at that time—we were even too cool for Tina Turner. That's why we had neglected to mention this part of the trip to our stoner friends.

But I loved Tina Turner and respected her many reinventions. From Anna Mae Bullock to celebrity punching bag to The Acid Queen to Hollywood Squares staple.[36] And now her comeback. Her rise from victim to superstar. I loved her. Kelly and I loved her. And we hated Ike turner. We would gladly let her do to us what he did to her if it would make her feel better or somehow take her pain away. I'd happily let her crush my hand beneath her stiletto if she needed to for some reason—who wouldn't?

We got there with plenty of time to spare and all the essentials: a sheet to spread on the grass, a large cooler filled with

[36] Tina played The Acid Queen in the movie version of the musical, *Tommy*. The Hollywood Squares was a game show where showbiz "personalities," minor celebrities, and famous people who had hit a bump in their careers, made sexual innuendos while playing tic-tac-toe. Paul Lynde was always the center square, and he was the funniest cast member. And apparently mean IRL. He famously said—or didn't say—to a mother with a crying baby on a plane: *Shut that kid up or I'm gonna fuck it.* He wasn't endearing.

vodka and orange juice, and two glasses stolen from the dining hall. And we started drinking. And we drank. And we drank. And we drank and we drank and we drank. Our livers were young, and so were we. And we barely glanced at the stage where Don Henley was singing his heart out. Again, we were way too cool to listen to him. Though I secretly loved his song and video "The Boys of Summer."

Sometimes even the people you keep secrets with, you keep secrets from.

And to pass the time, we played games. We told our nearest neighbors we were a couple from the New Hebrides, which is a place mentioned in my favorite movie *What's Up, Doc?*[37] And even though the New Hebrides are in Australia, we said we were Irish and tried to speak in an Irish accent which sounded vaguely Indian.

Carried away by the alcohol and the yarns we were spinning for this actual couple, Kelly playfully put her head in my lap. Even as drunk as I was, I knew I was playing a dangerous game. I had to put a stop to it and fast. It was wrong to play with someone's feelings. And suddenly, I knew I had to step up and make it right with Kelly no matter how hard it would be to tell the truth. But instead of that, I grabbed her and started making out with her, smacking our teeth together in a way that would've been extremely painful if we hadn't been soaked in booze from the brain down. And she reciprocated. Oh, we must've been a beautiful sight—two shit-faced college students rolling around on a dirty sheet, making out like drunken sailors.

And then…nothing. The next memory I had was of walking unsteadily through a large field. And everything was a little

[37] *What's Up, Doc?* is a perfect movie. If you don't agree, you're wrong.

blurry, and someone was calling my name. After a bit, I recognized her. Kelly! She rushed to me, and I rushed to her, and we fell into each other's arms and hugged like we thought we were the last people on Earth. And it seemed like we might be. It was dark and there wasn't a soul in sight. We looked around, panicked. What happened? Where were we?

And then it slowly dawned on us. The field where we stood was a full parking lot when we last saw it. Somehow it had become several hours later. And neither one of us could remember what had happened after Don Henley left the stage. At first, the answer seemed obvious: We had been abducted by a UFO and were suffering from lost time. There could be no other explanation. And I must have put up quite a fight. How else to explain the rips in both of the knees of my pants and the dirt and blood on the palms of my hands? And the twisted ankle I could barely walk on? The fact that Kelly didn't have her purse and not only was my wallet missing but the back pocket it had been in was ripped almost completely off, must have meant we were abducted by some sort of gang-y aliens who were tired of all the experimenting and probing and just wanted to make a quick buck.

And then Kelly promptly turned away and projectile vomited a stream of screwdrivers that would make an exorcist proud. And I began to suspect it was less alien and more of a blackout caused by the obscene amounts of screwdrivers we had consumed. And it appeared we had been robbed.

That was when things started to come slowly back to me. I began to have vague, unfocused images of sitting in a room and talking to an official-looking man who sat at a desk while another man stood nearby. And they were smiling and talking to me like I was a child as I attempted to communicate with them. I might have even been crying. Which I think made them laugh. And then the one standing leaned in uncomfortably close to my face and suddenly burst out laughing even harder.

And then, when the image went away, I realized why everything looked so blurry. I pulled off my glasses and found that the lenses were gone. I was only wearing frames.

We panicked even more. Somehow, we preferred alien abduction to being drunk and robbed. That's not a sexy story. And my favorite pants had been destroyed. They had a Velcro fly and were gathered at the ankle. I'd bought them years ago, how was I going to replace them? They were my "thing." I wore them with one red Converse and one green Converse. That was what I was known for. What would my "thing" be now?!

We tried to rally. We had to locate our car. But no matter where we looked, it was nowhere to be found. And then we spotted our savior—the tour bus. It was still parked outside the concert hall! Its windows were tinted and there was no one around but somehow, we knew, we just *knew*, that Tina Turner was on that bus. We were convinced she hadn't left yet. Maybe she needed to comb out her wig before they took off; it must be hard to do that when the bus is going over speed bumps or whatever. And surely, she would help us. How could she not? She understood trouble and pain. She once had to go on stage and perform after Ike had broken her jaw. She'd know what to do. And, as Kelly helpfully pointed out, I knew her! I just needed to remind her. (I think at this point, that was factual for me.)

So we ran up to the bus, and we knocked and knocked, and then we pounded and pounded. We called her name. "Tina! Tina! It's Jon! Jon and Kelly! Remember Jon? He gave you his jacket!" (That one came from Kelly.) "We came from Oswego! It's a state school on Lake Ontario! We drove all the way here to see you and got into a big mess! Help us! For chrissake, help us!"

It turned out we *did* need another hero.

But no one answered. Oh, we heard movement on the bus. We knew there were people on board. People who had decided to ignore us. We were also fairly certain that she was on board. I could have sworn I heard that familiar rasp saying the words "drunk fuckers." We realized she wasn't going to help us. We were on our own.

Eventually we found our car. It really wasn't that hard—it was the only one in the middle of another enormous field. And after several hours of drunken sleep, we puked some more and made our way back to Oswego. Kelly was too sick, so I drove home with my good left foot and limited vision.

When asked how the meeting with the politician guy went, we told people we felt we were heard, and then we went to bed for a few days.

At some point, my roommate Jerry made me listen to the many messages from my mother, each one more frantic than the next.[38] Apparently, at some point in the evening, I had called her crying and begged her to come get me, and then hung up. "But, where are you?" she kept saying on the machine. "You didn't tell me where you are!"

---

38 Answering machines were how you got phone messages from people. Those messages were recorded on cassettes. You left an outgoing message, such as: "We're not home, please leave a message," which might cause your mother to say, in her best impression of a criminal, "Oh, no one's home? Well, I'm a robber, and I think I'll just come over there and rob you right now." Click.

Kelly and I never spoke of the make out session. Given what happened, I wasn't even sure she remembered. We remained friends, but I eventually widened my circle.

I drifted into that receptacle of all that is weird and other—the theater department, where I could once again become someone else. Where lying was actually the whole point.

It wasn't until a few years after college that I decided to officially tell Kelly the truth about me. The Gay truth. All that other shit about being South African and not knowing my exact age had more or less been forgotten by the end of freshman year. She deserved the truth. I had made her pay for all the gas to see Tina Turner.

We met at Grand Central Oyster Bar. She had a few beers, but I didn't drink. By that point, I had learned to tell the truth sober and *then* drink to numb the pain of all that truth telling. Thinking I was being nice, I even said, "Well if I wasn't Gay, you would've been the one!" Her look said it all: *What a jackass.*

Then we put some Tina on the jukebox and drank, and drank some more. But not nearly as much as we used to. This was New York and it was way too expensive. And drunk people were vulnerable people.

As the saying goes: "Blackout rob me once, shame on you; blackout rob me twice, shame on me."

I felt something on the walk back to my apartment in the East Village. I think it was a good feeling. And I was pretty sure I felt that way because I had told the truth. I vowed never to lie again.

Then, just as I got to Thirteenth Street, a guy approached me and asked me if I was Jeffrey Combs. Well, I happened to know who Jeffrey Combs was—he had the lead in the indie horror film *Re-Animator* from a few years earlier. It was a movie

I loved. I smiled and was about to say the truth, but then he asked for my autograph. And I didn't hesitate for a second, I gave it to him. I signed as Jeffrey. I think signing an autograph—even if it's for someone you're not—is the one exception to the "always telling the truth" thing.

My Baboon Lover

The one time I got crabs was from a guy who had just had a heart transplant. His name was Dave. I met him at a former restaurant space on 14th Street in Manhattan where I volunteered to serve macrobiotic meals to people with HIV and AIDS. He was cute, with a big nose and thick hair. And skinny—the kind of skinny where you wondered if he was going to collapse any second. In short, he was the man of my dreams. He never missed a meal. And I never missed an opportunity to stare, practically willing him and his big nose to notice me.

Eventually, I caught him giving me the glad eye and I found the nerve to start a conversation. He told me that he qualified for the meal not based on his HIV status, which was negative, but because of his heart, which until a few months ago had belonged to someone else.

It turned out he shared this fact right away with everyone he met. It's a pretty great icebreaker, so I didn't blame him for leading off with it. Why bother going through something that traumatic unless you can immediately tell everyone you meet about it? It makes you infinitely more interesting. And unpredictable since there's always the possibility the heart will take on the murderous rage of the homicidal maniac it previously belonged to. And they always do at some point. Always.

I was coming off a particularly slutty period, having been dumped by my first real boyfriend, who wasn't nice to me. He broke up with me while we were working a brunch shift at Wylies, and I was resentful that I had to pool my tips with him at the end of the shift. I remember saying to him, "You're a bad person." (Years later, when Facebook happened, I decided to look him up, maybe say "hello." A lot of time had passed, and I thought it was time for closure. I had forgiven him. After all, we were both young and learning how to do the relationship thing. But when I saw his photo, he looked like he was wearing a toupee. And it's common knowledge that people who wear toupees are inherently bad, so he got no forgiveness from me.)

But I did enjoy dipping my toe into the slutty, sexy world of Gay New York. And that little toe-dip became a cannonball into the deep end. I was ready to have fun! But be careful. But have wild uninhibited nonstop boy fucking! But safely.

It was the era of "safe sex." Which became "safer sex," which was basically "safe sex" without having to pretend to use condoms for oral.

Well, I didn't really have to worry about anything safe with this guy. I had been skiing on the Matterhorn, and now I was at the top of the bunny slope.

We started dating but in the mildest form possible. He couldn't strain himself. He was too afraid of raising his heartbeat in any way, so all we did was kiss quick little pecks like children might. But I didn't mind since he was so cute and so interesting. And I could show him off like a prize pig at a county fair.

At parties, I would make him lift his shirt to expose the long scar running down the middle of his chest. I'd get mad when he insisted on telling people the boring truth about his donor—that she was a young housewife from New Jersey who was hit by a car. On my third Jack and Coke, I would tell people he was given a baboon heart as part of a secret government experiment. I'd describe how we'd be walking through Central Park when he'd suddenly dash up a tree and kill a squirrel, ripping it in half with his bare hands. I even started calling him "Ripper," thinking "Dave" was too boring, too "guy who has his original heart."

Before he had the surgery, he was an athlete and had excelled at several different sports. He had even played in the Gay Games, where he won medals for swimming. Which meant that skinny body might have more of a story to tell than I thought. And even though I found the Gay Games a little embarrassing—I mean they have competitions in male pair ice dancing (insert internalized homophobia here)—I could still live out my Mark Spitz fantasy. And what red-blooded male of a certain generation didn't have a Mark Spitz fantasy? Mark Spitz's mustache probably made more boys Gay than DNA and Barbra Streisand's disco phase combined.

He was hoping to be in the next games held in Amsterdam, but his little heart problem got in the way.

For someone who could drop dead if anyone so much as said "boo" to him, he was ambitious. He had decided that on the one-year anniversary of his operation, he would climb Mount Everest. He had the admirable goal of being the first heart transplant survivor to do this. He had been a mountain climber with his first heart, and Everest had been a long-term goal of his, but he also intended it to raise awareness of the importance of organ donation. And since I was smitten, I immediately signed up to be an organ donor. (Or I enthusiastically told him I was going to and then forgot, which sounds more like me.) He was trying to raise money for this endeavor by hosting an event at a Gay bar in the Village and asked if I would perform. Well, how could I say no? How could I do or say anything that might cause his new heart to break?

Now, I've always been a huge fan of the movie *What's Up, Doc?*[39] So much so that I bought a plaid bowtie and matching cummerbund exactly like the one the character played by Ryan O'Neal has in the movie, and wore it to my prom. My good friend John loved the movie too, so we decided the two of us would lip-synch the song "You're the Top," which is sung by Ryan and Barbra Streisand over the end credits. Naturally, I was Ryan since I had the tie and cummerbund. And John found a dress and a wig and—god help us—a pair of big nose and glasses, like the kind you find at a novelty shop, with the bushy eyebrows removed, of course. Barbra didn't really perform in thick black glasses, but what the fuck? It was a tacky Gay bar—how hard were we supposed to work? And besides the glasses were necessary to keep the extremely offensive nose on his face. We had no choice.

Well, the night was not a success. Ten people held ten matching looks of horror as we lip-synched badly and rushed off the stage to anemic applause. I think we raised thirty dollars. But it didn't matter. The important thing was that we tried. And the *more* important thing was that I persuaded Dave/Ripper to drink a bit of beer, and there was a distinct possibility I might get a little something that night.

[39] I can't stress enough what a good movie *What's Up, Doc?* is.

Well, my gambit paid off, and I was promptly rewarded with a trip back to my place, where I carefully went all the way with my Lil' Ripper. It was finally his turn to donate an organ.

And he may have been HIV negative, but he was certainly crabs positive, since I found myself itching uncontrollably shortly thereafter. And that about did it for us. After I mentioned this to him, he insisted he got them from a massage table, and I believed him. But he stopped coming to the healthy meals I helped serve, and I never heard from him again. I guess he was too embarrassed.

And I didn't really mind. I was beginning to think that his lack of passion was due to the fact that he was a total bore and not because of his brand-new housewife heart.

Now whenever I get an itch anywhere near my bathing suit area, I think of him. I wonder if he ever climbed that mountain. It's hard for me to imagine him being that active. I can only see him in a kitchen in New Jersey, wiping his hands on his apron as he puts dinner on the table for his husband, nervous that the roast will be dry.

And I suppose the lesson is: you only get two hearts in this life. Make sure the second one comes with a sexy, dangerous backstory. And then live your life to honor it.

What I Did For Love

I would like it to be known that I am not a Streisand queen. Not anymore, that is. Oh sure, like any normal red-blooded American, self-loathing, uncoordinated white Gay boy, I worshipped her growing up. For the usual reasons: She was an outsider, she was different, she had to make her own way, blah blah blah. All of that is true, but none of it mattered at the time. All that mattered was my love for her. I saw myself in her, connected to her on a cellular level.

I've heard that if the queen bee dies, all her bees die with her. They are that connected. Would it be the same if something—god forbid—happened to Barbra? I suppose we will find out in the not-too-distant future, with queens across the world dropping like flies, or in this case, bees. But in those days, such thoughts were far from my head, which was only filled with all things Barbra. I watched her movies, and I read every magazine article about her I could, eating up delicious word after word. And, yes, I may have even checked her French album *Je m'appelle Barbra* out of the public library, hiding it in a Sears shopping bag. I may have been smitten, but I wasn't an idiot.

Once her version of *A Star Is Born*, was released in 1976, my adoration grew to a terrifying frenzy. To the sad few who don't know, Barbra's version of *A Star Is Born* is the story of a drugged out, washed up rock star named John Norman Howard, played by the very hot Kris Kristofferson, and the up-and-coming singer who eclipses him, Esther Hoffman, played, of course, by La Streisand. He sees her potential and helps give her the confidence she needs to succeed. But the higher her star rises while singing bad pop songs written by Paul Williams,[40] the more he can't take it. He drinks a lot of Jack Daniels and eventually crashes his sporty car in the desert, killing his hot self. Barbra has a fabulous scene at the crash site where she breaks down sobbing uncontrollably, but her nails look so perfect you just know she'll survive.

I had to see it. But the problem was it was rated R. And somehow watching it late, late at night scrambled on the Home Box Office channel that we didn't subscribe to just wasn't enough. So I rode my bike to the Hollywood Theater in Mattydale, New York, snuck in the exit door when the earlier showing was letting out, and waited in the men's room until it was time for the next show. What innocent times those were—when a ten-year-old boy could hang out in a men's room in a discount movie theater for forty minutes and live to tell the tale.

A Star Is Born was playing on a double feature with *Lady Sings the Blues*, a biopic about Billie Holiday.[41] And even though it was fun seeing Diana Ross in a straitjacket with insanity hair,

[40] Paul Williams wrote a lot of pop songs in the '70s. You can look him up. But you also don't have to.

[41] Billie Holiday, nicknamed "Lady Day," was an amazing jazz singer in the '40s and '50s. Her vocal style, strongly influenced by jazz instrumentalists, inspired a new way of manipulating phrasing and tempo. She was a genius, and openly bi. Everyone should know who she is.

swallowing handfuls of pills and scenery, it wasn't what I went there to see. Oddly, Barbra had her own version of insanity hair in her movie. It was a sort of Harpo Marx afro given to her by her then-boyfriend, hair stylist-turned-producer, Jon Peters. I still remember a particularly harsh review of the movie: "Jon Peters may have done wonders with Barbra's hair, but he left her career with a serious case of split ends." I think I wrote that critic a letter in defense of her hair. I think I used the word "umbrage."

I loved every ridiculous moment of that movie. But it was more than mere entertainment to me. It was a watershed moment in my life. At the end, when Barbra steps out on stage in a tribute to her hot dead husband and says very simply, "I'm Esther Hoffman Howard," I was transcended. It was an important moment. It was the moment a bit of diffused light appeared under the door of the dark, dark closet I lived in.

I must have sat through that movie a dozen more times. I bought the album, copied the cover for an art class assignment, and dreamed of remaking it. With myself in the lead. It had been remade a lot, so I figured why not, one day, with me.

And I knew I wanted to be an actor.

My way of pursuing my dream of becoming a famous actor was an unorthodox one: I kept it in my head and never did anything about it.

But it's not as if I let go of the dream. It consumed me. And I was sure it would happen. Just as sure as I was that I would do nothing to help make it happen. I knew I was good, and for some reason that felt enough. So I bided my time. Waited to be discovered. And I managed to get through junior high and high school not only without acting but without really speaking at all.

At college, I decided the time was right to let the world finally see what I had known for years—that I was the greatest performer in the world. That I could sing, dance, and do any accent called for. In my mind, I could even fence. I graciously agreed to play a messenger in a scene from a Shakespeare play for a directing class. I was nervous and tripped over my cape, but it went *okay*.[42] And I actually got discovered. Sort of.

One of the acting teachers, Ron Medici, a small Gay man with a big Gay mustache, asked me to audition for *A Chorus Line*, the upcoming main stage production. I was terrified, but somehow found the nerve to sign up. I made the decision the way I made all important decisions—drunk. I auditioned with a monologue I found about an old man at the end of his life remembering how he survived the Holocaust. Well, this eighteen-year-old from Syracuse must have made the horrors of Auschwitz very real for Ron, because, to my surprise, he cast me in the plum role of Paul, the Puerto Rican drag queen. (The idea of cultural appropriation still hadn't hit white people just yet.)

Paul is a great part. He doesn't sing much—thank god—but he has this huge long monologue about working in a shitty Times Square theater as a drag queen. His parents, of course, don't understand him, and he's so femmy, he's basically shunned by his father. One day at work, he comes out in full drag and runs right into his parents, who have come into the city to say goodbye to him before he goes on tour. He is mortified; they

[42] I later stole this cape—as well as a pirate shirt and a pair of "period boots" from the costume department—after I played Petruchio in *Taming of the Shrew* my senior year at Oswego. You'll meet them again when I make my triumphant return to the role later in New York. Did I know I was destined to play Petruchio again? Sure, why not?

didn't know exactly what his job was. They are stunned. After an awkward moment, his father tells him to make sure he eats enough. Then he tells the stage manager to take care of his son. It's this incredible moment for Paul. His father had never called him *son* before. And then Paul breaks down crying, alone on stage. I had to do this part. I *had* to play that sad Puerto Rican drag queen. And I had just the mustache to do it.

Our production was the first college production allowed after the Broadway production and national tours, so we felt as if we had a lot resting on our shoulders. And it didn't help that on day one of rehearsal Ron looked us up and down and said, "Jesus Christ, people, lay off the chips!" We frantically tried to get into shape and lose all the college beer weight we had put on. I remember joking that maybe we should change the title to *A Cafeteria Line*. And instead of singing, "What I Did for Love," we could sing "What I Had For Lunch."

The day after the cast list went up, reality set in. I was going to have to sing and dance in front of all my stoner friends. In *tights*! And the more we got into rehearsals, the more I began to fear that I couldn't actually sing, dance, or act. Was it possible I was not the triple threat that I had been in my head? What in god's name had I gotten myself into?

Rehearsals were hard. Like Vietnam hard. And Ron was not someone to sugar coat things. "Jesus Christ, people! That's not a circle! I don't know what the hell that is! And you're supposed to *dance* out from the wings, not schlep out like you've got a load in your pants. And smile, you all look constipated!" It wouldn't have served anyone to point out the contradictory images he was creating. He was like Debbie Allen from *Fame* in the body of a Super Mario Brother.[43] Who could do a split. I can still see him, one hand on his hip, the other pulling frantically at the front of his hair, pacing back and forth. It was like watching Napoleon trying to decide what to order at a deli that had limited choices.

I was a nervous wreck. Whenever I had to sing my little part in rehearsal, I would leave my body and watch myself as I somehow warbled through it. Whenever I hit a note, it was an accident. And there was resentment from some of the cast. Who was this young upstart? This undeclared major? Everyone else in the cast had been in plays before, had actually performed on a stage at some point and not just in the black box theater where the classes were taught. One of the actors who wanted the part of Paul drew the poster for the production, and deliberately made me fat in it. I went around campus making myself thinner with a sharpie.

In desperation, I tried pointing out to Ron other guys who might be able to jump right in and take my part, but I was met with a stern, "Fuck that!"

I tried to barter with him. Could I maybe talk through my song like Rex Harrison or Neil Diamond?[44] "Fuck that!"

So I had no choice but to dive in and give it my all. I skipped classes to rehearse on my own. I practiced hitting the notes whenever I thought no one was around. I switched to lite beer. I watched my hairline recede from stress. I had my own practice montage.

---

[43] Debbie Allen is a dancer, actor, and choreographer who has a famous line in the movie *Fame*. Was there a remake? Was she in it? Did she say the line again? Does anyone know? Does anyone care?

[44] Rex Harrison was in *My Fair Lady*. Neil Diamond is a pop star from the '70s and '80s. They both talk-sang. Interesting fact: *My Fair Lady* sucks. Prove me wrong!

Opening night finally came. And everyone in the cast had family coming. Except me. And it was sort of my fault. I'd only ever given my family tidbits about my life and decided *Chorus Line* would be no different. I sort of half told them I was doing it, and they sort of half heard me. And we all knew how this arrangement would work: They would never mention it again and I would be fine with that. I guess I was a little like Paul, embarrassed about what I was doing. I couldn't have them come see me sing and dance and talk about being Gay and a drag queen. It would raise questions I would still rather leave unasked.

It was five minutes to curtain, and I remember Tara Biederman saying to me, "Paul is such a hard part—it's where the intermission would normally be. The audience is restless. Break a leg!"

Of course, this sent me crying to Ron, my eyeliner running. "I can't do it, Ron! I can't do it!"

He pulled me aside and said in his no bullshit way, "You can do it. Did you think I cast you because you're cute? Well, I did. But I also knew you could do it. Why would I give the best part to someone who isn't talented? I would look like an asshole. Jon, I don't like to look like an asshole." Then he told me to look in the dressing room.

And for a moment I thought: *Oh my god, my parents are there to wish me luck, just like Paul's!* But it wasn't my parents. It was a huge bouquet of flowers sent by Ron and Emily and Eric, two of the cast members I had become close with. It was signed, "With Sincere Sympathy: The Executive Committee." I was moved beyond words. And it gave me the confidence I needed to drag my Danskin-covered ass on stage.

Well, I did my monologue, and it went fine. I didn't set the world on fire, but I didn't want to kill myself either. But poor Paul is not off the hook even then. Shortly after he spills his guts to the director, he falls and hurts his knee, a fate worse than death to a dancer. Sad. But happy again when he comes back to lead the cast in the final number "One." Waiting in the wings for my cue, I saw this as my Esther Hoffman Howard moment, and I seized it for all it was worth. And by that, I mean I didn't fuck it up.

The show went well, and I got a few compliments from my stoner friends. And I saw my future begin to coalesce. This production of *A Chorus Line* was my coming out as an actor. And closely followed by my coming out as Gay to Ron, the one person I felt safe to tell. I remember being drunk and ugly crying in his living room one night after the show. "I think I'm Gay!" I'm pretty sure I used the word "umbrage" then too. He was very helpful and sympathetic, even though he probably just felt like saying, "Really? You're Gay?! Quelle surprise!" I got the feeling he had played this scene before.

There are many coming-outs in one's life. Coming out to yourself being the first. But saying it out loud may be the most important.

It felt like the world's heaviest weight had been lifted off my shoulders. I gradually came to feel like a different person. There was me before and me after. I was still filled with fear and shame and devoid of self-esteem, but I stood a bit straighter and was unafraid of wearing brighter colors.

Then, of course, there are the other coming-outs: your family, your friends, your dealer (risky and unnecessary, not sure why I did it), and so on. And then all the little micro–coming outs that follow you the rest of your life. I still feel a little bit nervous if I have to say "my husband" to a credit card person on the phone. If they hate Queers, they could fuck with your finances and feel they're doing God's work.

I'd like to add one more: coming out to a sex worker. Several years ago, when Sunset Boulevard was still a bit sketchy, I was exiting the Rite Aid just as a clearly gacked-out sex worker was walking past. "You want some company?" she slurred. I don't know why, but I smiled and said, "I don't think my boyfriend would appreciate that," to which she replied, "Well, you tell him he one lucky faggot."

I recently bought the DVD of *A Star Is Born* and watched it with the commentary. Barbra couldn't seem more detached and unfocused. Anyone looking for insight would be sorely disappointed. All she seems to want to talk about are the clothes. You can almost picture her sitting on her couch in a comfortable flowy, caftan-y thing, which matches everything else in the room, swirling a glass of chardonnay as she ruminates on her film. "Oh, that poncho was nice. Bought it in Sedona, I think. Or was it Santa Fe? Oh, my hair looks good there. Oh, I still have those stretch pants. Oh, I just love all the turquoise." I imagined her in thick black glasses.

It got me thinking. When they release the SUNY Oswego version of *A Chorus Line* on DVD—and they will—I hope I'm asked to do commentary. I will wear a flowy, caftan-y thing as well, and I will swirl a wine cooler, making comments such as, "Oh, he missed that step. Oh, her leotard is riding up her ass. Oh, my package looks good! Oh, I'm off key. I think. 'Who Am I Anyway?'—well, we know I'm not a singer!" But mostly I will talk about my acting teacher, director, mentor and friend Ron Medici.

For me, he was John Norman Howard, Debbie Allen, guardian angel, and fairy godmother rolled into one compact Italian man.

I'd like to think that if your parents don't understand you or give you what you need, something (the Universe? Does that even exist? I have my doubts.) will provide someone who does. Someone who sees something in you that you don't. Someone who arrives in your life just when you need them. To give you whatever it is you need to keep going. Someone who shows up with a key when you are faced with many locked doors. And Ron was that person for me.

A Chorus Line was a pivotal moment in my life. I learned I could be adequate in a musical! Yay! And after several years of doing this and that, I realized my acting career really peaked with that show. And that was okay because it allowed everything else in my life to happen. Thanks to Ron, there was a possibility that I could become one singular sensation every little step I took.

The Tour of Dying Parents

Years ago, I was having coffee with my friend Amy and I told her my mother had Alzheimer's. "That's awful. I'm so sorry," she said. "Does that mean you have to come out to her every time you see her?" Alzheimer's humor. Nothing funny about it to most, but my mother would have laughed. At that point, she wouldn't even get the joke because, well, she had Alzheimer's. And, yes, I've had to come out to her again and again. Nature's cruel. Not only does she lose her memory, she has to be disappointed by her Gay son a handful of times in one weekend.

When it seemed as though his own mother wasn't doing very well, and the end might be near, Chris and I went on what we jokingly referred to as The Tour of Dying Parents. We think we're funny that way. We laugh in the face of death. Especially if it's not coming for us. It was a short tour, and we only played two dates: Indianapolis, where he had escaped from, and then Syracuse, where *I* had.

Virginia had gone into the hospital for cancer treatment, and like lots of Gay guys, he is preternaturally attached to her.

An oddly tall eighty-something, she laid in her bed at the nursing home, recovering from chemo and radiation, with her feet hanging off the end of the bed. She was what we would now call "a bad ass." But that part of her seemed to be slipping away. The only thing she wanted was a Frosty from Wendy's and her stuffed animal—a cat called Little Monster. Chris has to complain about the TV in her room—it seemed to play nothing but *Cops* all day and she lived in a constant state of fear that the hospital was under attack.

It was Christmas Eve, and we had dinner with his family. I sat next to his dad, who was on oxygen and connected to a tank by little hoses in his nose. I found that when I talked to him, my breathing would take on a pace similar to his, struggling for oxygen until I thought I would pass out onto the platter of cold cuts.

His family was not exactly the healthiest family in the world. And neither was mine. We used to joke that if we were able to conceive a child somehow, which I would give birth to because eating and complaining are my two favorite things, the kid would have a scary gene pool. They'd probably love cats and female rock stars but at some point, they'd have to choose between alcoholism, depression, cancer, and Alzheimer's. Or any combination of those. We would hope for a girl, so, as she's making her way through the buffet of illnesses, she wouldn't also have to leave room on her plate for male-pattern baldness. We both have that in our family, too.

Not long ago we went to a wig party at a friend's house. Chris wore a shoulder-length blond sort of California surfer wig, and I opted for a long red one with bangs that I thought was very British '60s model but turned out to be more '80s hair band. We had fun, and on the way home, Chris joked that wig parties are a good idea because they could help prepare you for when you get cancer and have to wear one. I don't think we should live our lives expecting the worst, but I do think laughing at cancer and Alzheimer's and any other illness can somehow make them less powerful. Billy Wilder once said, "Life is terrible, but it's not that serious."[45]

It's a valuable lesson I learned from my late boyfriend Luis, whose picture magnet is currently stuck to my bedside lamp. He was very involved in AIDS activism both in front of and behind the scenes. I, on the other hand, was a foot soldier. Someone who only wanted to be told where to go and who to scream at. It was therapy for me at a time when I couldn't afford it. Because he volunteered with ACT UP, worked for an AIDS research project, and had known many people with HIV and AIDS, his diagnosis of leukemia came out of left field.

It was a strange thing at that time—a Gay guy getting leukemia. It just wasn't on anybody's list of must-have diseases. It seemed like something for straight people or cats. And we both felt very unprepared for it. Me more than him. He found himself having to go from chemo to healing sessions with his doctor to taking care of me, assuring me everything was going to be alright and holding me while I cried and played "Why" by Annie Lennox over and over and over.

He adjusted quickly, however, and the joy and laughter with which he viewed everything in life soon spread to his illness. He never stopped fighting it, and he never stopped laughing at it. The only time I remember him upset was when he wasn't sure if

[45] Billy Wilder was the director of such amazing films as *Double Indemnity*, *Sunset Boulevard*, *Some Like It Hot*, and many others. According to Computer, he wasn't Gay, though Wikipedia describes him as "a terrific dancer, a womanizer, and a wit." You decide.

he'd get out of the hospital in time to perform as Linda Ronstadt at a benefit that night. But he made it, and after I helped him tape down the catheter, which we hid under his peasant blouse, he took the stage as Linda in her Mexican phase, lip-synching to "Por un Amor," from her album *Canciones de Mi Padre*. Songs of My Father. It brought the casa down.

After he passed, I vowed Luis's memorial needed to be a testament to who he was and what he would want. I knew he wouldn't want tears and sad remembrances. In that case, the cancer would have won. No, in order for Luis to win, it had to be a party.

So, on a night when New York was experiencing one of the worst snowstorms in decades, a hundred or so people gathered at the Manhattan Center For Living on Lower Broadway in full-on drag to say goodbye. Boys came as girls. Girls came as boys. Girls came as much girlier versions of themselves. Boys did too. My outfit was simple: A black dress with some tasteful lace around the bottom, pearls, and a white Barbara Bush wig, which looked better on me than on her. I was the grieving widow. With a costume change, of course, for my performance. I had a really great '50s suit à la Nat King Cole, and Luis and I—well, a blown-up cardboard cutout of Luis with a manipulatable mouth—lip-synced to "Unforgettable," by Natalie Cole and her dead father. It was our song.

There were some great performances that night, including my friend Paul, a Patti LaBelle fanatic with a few extra pounds, who tore it up as "Beef Patty." And my friend Tom made a particularly memorable Stevie Nicks, playing guitar and singing in a just a wig, shawl, jockstrap. At the end of the evening, we let a giant cardboard wig, held aloft by balloons, loose in the street. It sort of bobbed up and down a bit as if it weren't quite ready to go, then suddenly rose up and took off over Manhattan. Hopefully, wherever it landed, Luis was there to release the turtles it probably trapped.[46]

My parents never got to meet Luis. At first because I wasn't ready, and later, well, he died, and that point became moot. It wasn't as if I was let off the hook though. As hard as it may be for parents to accept the idea of a live boyfriend for their son, it's even harder explaining a dead one. But my mom surprised me, calling me in New York and asking to speak to Luis's mother, who had come from San Francisco to stay with me and be near her son in his final days.

As I saw it, that was a heroic meeting of two women forced to be more remarkable than they ever knew they were capable of.

Christmas morning. Syracuse. The last stop on our tour. Before we went to see my father, Chris and I stopped at my mom's nursing home, but it was much too late. She was alive, but it was still too late. Chris would never get to meet my mother. They were in the same room, but she was missing. There was a dullness in her eyes and a smoothness to her face that broke my heart. There was no longer a trace of her.

She liked to laugh. And she was the most opinionated person I knew, every one of them wrong—meaning the opposite of mine. "Kill 'em all and let God sort 'em out!" was one of her mantras. Mostly, I think, it was just to get a rise out of me. She liked to be provocative and thought of herself as bawdy, flipping the bird to anyone whenever she felt like it. It was her bit. "Your mom's funny," my friends would say. But I was only embarrassed by her, rolling my eyes and rarely laughing at anything she said. "Laugh, it's funny," she would scold me. Humor

---

[46] Annie Lennox, Linda Ronstadt, Natalie Cole, Patty LaBelle, Stevie Nicks—DIVAS! The only true religion!

was her defense, and she passed that quality to me. And though I spent many distant, angry years trying to forgive her for other things, I am grateful for that.

She stopped laughing a long time ago. Alzheimer's had taken that away. It doesn't have a sense of humor. Or good timing. Several years, shrinks, and antidepressants later, I was at a place where I was ready to know her better and have her finally know me. But she was having trouble remembering who her husband was, calling 911 on the "stranger" in her house so many times the sheriff didn't respond anymore.

"AT MY AGE, I'VE SEEN IT ALL, DONE IT ALL, AND HEARD IT ALL. I JUST CAN'T REMEMBER IT ALL." This was on the coffee mug I drank decaf out of at my parent's house. Chris, my dad, and I were going to have lunch with my mom at the nursing home. As we got ready, my dad sat at the kitchen table, silently chain smoking his way to another heart attack he wouldn't tell his kids about, and Chris was studying the extensive collection of refrigerator magnets my mother had hoarded over the years. One was a plastic pack of cigarettes that, when pressed, made an annoying coughing sound. I pressed it several times—as I always did—and the hacking followed us out the door as we went to our first stop, Dunkin' Donuts, which served my mom's favorite coffee (black) and donuts (plain).

Chris and I made conversation as my father looked out the window and my mother sat in her wheelchair, eating her two plain donuts and staring at nothing. Needless to say, it was a depressing place, and all of the taped-up pictures of Snoopy in a Santa hat was not going to change that. A volunteer came over and said to my mother in that volunteer voice, "Make sure you save room for lunch, Eleanor!" As he walked away, my mother gave him the finger. My father scowled but Chris and I found this hysterical, and we laughed like idiots until someone shushed us. I guess we were disrupting the vibe.

After our tour, when we were relaxing at home in LA, we noticed that the little orange tree we'd planted in the backyard, and under which we had scattered some of Luis's ashes, had a small orange growing on it. We cut it up and each ate a piece, and it was the sweetest orange we'd ever tasted. But then Chris ruined the moment by wondering if we could get leukemia that way. We got a little grossed out and threw the rest down the disposal. It just felt too weird to eat your dead boyfriend.

Creeping on Madonna

I watched Madonna dance to her own song, and she had no idea I was there.

We had just finished shooting a scene from a *Will & Grace* episode and were moving onto the next. At that time, there were a lot of big names who wanted to be on the show, but this was a *huge* big one—Madonna. I guess she thought that if a lot of famous people wanted to be a part of it, then she should too.

As the crew began to set up for the scene, which took place in the apartment of Madonna's character, I slipped behind a flat to get a moment to myself. Shoot nights were too noisy for me. The audience was always in a frenzy—it was like being at a rock concert but not having the required drugs to enjoy it. Their screaming jumped to ear-damaging levels when "Borderline" began blasting over the speakers. I was happy to be alone. But then I noticed I wasn't.

Madonna was about ten feet away. She didn't see me—she was standing behind the door to her "apartment," waiting for her entrance and dancing. She was dancing to her own song.

And I was the only one who knew! I was getting my own private Madonna concert. She was smiling, really enjoying herself. And I loved her for that. For dancing to her own song and doing it with such joy and not needing anyone to be seeing it. It felt so un-Madonna like. And I felt like I was intruding on a very private moment. Not that Madonna ever had private moments. But I couldn't stop staring at her, as if I might figure her out. This woman who seemed to always know what she wanted and just went out and got it. Like she said, "I'm going to be a pop star," and became one. Then she said, "I'm going to be a Broadway star," and became one. Well, no. But she did a Broadway show, then made movies, and was now doing a sitcom. Did she ever question herself and her abilities? I don't think she did.

As I watched her do her patented '80s moves, I wondered where she got her confidence, her self-esteem, from. Was she born fully formed this way? It seemed like she must've been. Like she was Madonna even before she was Madonna. She had the gene. And that made me have *feelings* because I knew I didn't. My admiration turned to jealousy and resentment, as it always does. I had the impulse to yell, "Stop that!" at her, but thankfully, I didn't.

Why wasn't I born with self-esteem like Madonna?!

"Light out here, lights on over there!"

That was the extent of direction we got from our director during rehearsals for *Taming of the Shrew* in New York in the sweaty summer of 1989. I had gotten the lead role of Petruchio! It was exciting to get cast in something—anything—but that excitement was tempered by the fact that I auditioned for it in a sketchy, empty building on Forty-Second Street in front of a sketchy, empty man wearing a dirty T-shirt that read: "A Man's Gotta Believe in Something—I Believe I'll Have Another

Beer!" But fuck it, a part is a part. Even if it meant hearing the constant tinkling of crack vials as they were crushed under my feet on the way to rehearsals.

This was long before the Disney-fication of Times Square and the Gay-ification of Hell's Kitchen. It was actually kind of a cool old building with an old-timey elevator, many empty rooms, and tarps hung up randomly so there were all kinds of neat places to be murdered. But the play was not going to be mounted in the building. Oh, no. This was to be an outdoor production. In the back. Which was a parking lot. With a circle of wide cement borders where the action would take place and where the audience would sit.

We were to act among the audience, as if they were citizens of Verona or some shit like that. Interactive, if you will. To this day, that word makes my every orifice clench. It was Shakespeare in the Parking Lot. I remember thinking: I'm an actor, I'm supposed to be able to create magic anywhere! Why wouldn't people flock to see a production of *Taming of the Shrew* sitting on cement blocks in a parking lot where the occasional homeless person would walk through? Which happened. It did. A homeless man walked through the "stage area" muttering to himself and interrupting my speech in which I woo the "shrewish" Kate:

> "Thus in plain terms: your father hath consented
> That you shall be my wife, your dowry 'greed on,
> And, will you, nill you, I will marry you!"

"Don't do it—he sounds like an asshole."

Normally, someone who did that would've been removed, but he made up one third of the audience, and he did get the only laugh of the night. And at least he was alive. Unlike the corpse of the pigeon that appeared before a performance and remained untouched even though I complained to the "director" about it. But an actor in New York learns to get things done themselves, and I kicked the bird corpse with my "period" boots off the "stage" and onto the sidewalk where I passed it three nights a week on my way to the show. We learned that complaining accomplished nothing. Our headshots periodically fell from the bulletin board and onto the floor until one of the actors would put them back up. Near the end of the production, morale had become so low, we would just step on them as we made our way silently out the back door to bring Shakespeare to the masses—or mass—once again.

On closing night, our dressing room was robbed. Well, the area behind a tarp that was set up for us to keep our backpacks stored, was robbed. Though he denied it, I suspected the "director" believed he needed more than just "another" beer and needed our money to buy them.

Madonna wouldn't have taken the Shakespeare gig. She would never have allowed herself to be treated so shabbily. I told myself I was just "honing my craft," paying my dues. But I secretly suspected I was just taking any crumbs that were thrown my way—and should be happy that I was even offered them.

For several months after that soul draining experience, I would see that pigeon corpse as I was on my way somewhere, maybe to an audition. Probably on rollerblades. It had gotten smashed down flat somehow, more and more every time I saw it. Eventually, it became a kind of pigeon stain on the sidewalk. It made me sad to think that I was the only one who knew what that stain used to be. And to know that he or she gave their life for the theater.

No, self-esteem and confidence—the things that allowed Madonna to play Evita when we all knew she shouldn't—were not acquaintances of mine. I was like my favorite toy as a kid—an Etch A Sketch.[47] If something positive happened to me—if a guy checked me out or someone told me my hair looked good—I could etch a picture of "Confident Me." But that night, the screen would get shaken, and the image would disappear and have to be started again the next day.

Being an actor requires a belief in yourself. It's almost as important than talent—actually more. And I knew I didn't have the former, and I was starting to see how it affected the latter.

I often wondered if I was on the wrong path. Was I just trying to be an actor because I was young and Gay and it was expected of me? Did I only get the part of Petruchio because I had the cape, pirate shirt, and boots that I stole from the costume department at SUNY Oswego? In which I also played Petruchio? Was I destined to forever be linked to this role and not allowed to take other parts? Oh, why couldn't the public see me any other way?!

Was it possible I wasn't good? I thought I was, but not enough people told me I was, and it takes a certain number of people to tell you something before you can believe it to be true. That's math.

And it *seemed* like I really wanted it. Like all struggling actors, I worked like a dog to finance my career. I waited tables, I handed out flyers for a florist in midtown dressed like a giant rose. A homeless man sitting on cardboard outside the store said: "You must feel like a real asshole." (Was it the same

---

[47] An Etch A Sketch is a toy with a screen to draw on that can be shaken, causing what was drawn to disappear. Great for kids to draw dirty pictures or write swear words and quickly shake it when a grown up approaches.

homeless man from *Taming of the Shrew*? Did he recognize me? Did he think I was good enough to stalk?) I made my friend Charlie come with me to pick up older men at a hustler bar on the Upper East Side, where I tried so hard to talk a white-haired gentleman into taking us both home that he said, "It sounds like *you* want to fuck your friend." Well, to diffuse that awkward moment, I promptly went to that gentleman's apartment and permitted him to pay me for sex. He lived in Sutton Place, so I felt like a high-priced call girl. Like Barbra Streisand in *Nuts*. That gave me a short boost of confidence.

I realized I needed help. At one point, I joined an actor's support group, which had the goal of empowering struggling actors. And which led me to chasing a casting director through the parking lot under Lincoln Center to ask for an audition for the national tour of *Six Degrees of Separation*. To my surprise, I got the audition. But that didn't go any further. Maybe I should've surprised her from her backseat to get a callback.

There was the occasional acting job, so I must've been doing *something* right.

Somehow, I got a part in a touring musical of *A Christmas Carol*, playing Bob Cratchit. Maybe it was my inability to sing or do a passable British accent that somehow charmed them into casting me. It wasn't glamorous. We had to unload and reload that goddamn truck as we pulled in and out of theaters in cities all over the Midwest and Northeast. And the show itself wasn't easy, either. At one point, I had to lift Tiny Tim up and put him on my shoulder. Only our Tim wasn't a he, our Tim was a she. A girl who was older than we all thought and had a bit of a growth spurt during the tour. By the end, I was afraid for my back and was extremely conscious of where I put my hands while lifting her. One cool thing that came out of that gig was meeting convicted serial killer Caril Ann Fugate, who came to opening night at the Lincoln Community Playhouse in Lincoln, Nebraska. I was thrilled to meet her—I think I gushed. She complimented my performance, so why wouldn't I?

But even compliments from serial killers weren't enough to get me to believe in myself.

The brief excitement of having a legit acting job didn't provide the self-esteem boost I needed. And as soon as I got back, my Etch A Sketch erased me, and I went back to the crumbs. The student films, where they pay you in pizza. An extra dressed in fetish wear in an ad on Manhattan Cable. "Call 976-PEEE—the extra E is for extra pee."[48] Honing my craft. Always honing. Honing, honing, honing.

And my proudest achievement, Loud Blouse, like all comedy groups, eventually dissolved in a haze of substance abuse, egos, glitter, and blackmail. But, really, we were all just too broke.

I was finding it harder and harder to keep trying. I needed some outside assurance that I was on the right path.

I decided that since I couldn't see my future, maybe someone else could. And since I didn't have Caril Ann Fugate's number—I doubt she was listed—I decided to ask my friend Steve to tell me what it was. He had gone to Yale for acting, which meant he was the real deal. He knew things. I took him to lunch and demanded he tell me the truth: Would I make it as an actor? I was very direct—I told him I wanted an honest

[48] Manhattan Cable was a local cable channel that played content so bad it was not to be missed. Former porn star Robin Byrd hosted a show in which she sang "Baby Let Me Bang Your Box" and pretended to put her guests' penises in her eye. This was real.

opinion, and I swore I would be grateful for whatever he told me. And always love and respect him. Of course, being a human being, he refused to answer. But I begged and pleaded and wore him down until finally, "No, I don't. I don't think you will make it as an actor!" It was a gut punch. And through tears, I hissed at him that he was a monster—how could he say something so awful? And I left him with the check.

But I knew he was right. It wasn't going to happen.

I took a job at a medical magazine. They needed to know if I would be there for at least a year, since they had hired performers who would take the job and then leave with little or no notice. I told them, yes, I would be there a while. I was giving up acting.

During my time there, I was never really sure what my job was, except it involved using this novel thing called "email," which I found kind of cool. I spent a lot of time flipping through those medical magazines. I remember the articles about advanced STIs. And the pictures. The pictures. Holy Christ, the *pictures.* Those I will never forget. And neither will the friends who saw them in the magazines I smuggled out. The genitals that were no longer recognizable as genitals. And I thought: *This is my life now: staring at someone's junk that resembles baked cauliflower.*

Then Tracy called. She had moved to LA to help her friend, Michael Patrick King, on the pilot he had written. Would I like to come? Maybe we can try our hands at writing TV?

Well, unlike Madonna and her reinventions, I wasn't going to change. I thought to myself: *Sure, I'll write.* But that was really just an excuse to find success as an actor…in LA! The problem wasn't me—it was New York! It just had too many mean homeless people and unintimidating casting directors in it.

Well, LA wasn't much different. I catered instead of waitered. I auditioned a lot—one time for a porno, "Would you be into being gangbanged?" "Um…can I wear a mask?" I didn't get a call back then, either.

I turned back to my old standby—sex work. I picked up an older gentleman at a hustler bar called Numbers in West Hollywood (which I think is a pizza parlor today). After our tryst, I would often see him at various performances I went to. It turned out he was a reviewer for a local theater newspaper. I wondered if he had mentally reviewed me, and how many stars I got.

I worked in a casting office, which was fascinating but sometimes sad. Michael Cole, so young and hot in the '70s show *The Mod Squad*, would call almost every day and ask if there was something—anything—he could come in and audition for. I used to jerk off to him, now I was dodging his calls. Hollywood.

While catering at the Governor's Ball after the Academy Awards ceremony, just as I was getting Robin Williams a Diet Coke, I was pulled from working on the floor because the manager spotted the tape that held my glasses together. Not only was I not going to win an Academy Award, I was kicked out of the afterparty. (Later, when Tracy and I worked with Robin Williams on *The Crazy Ones*, I thought of asking him if he remembered that, but decided he had probably gotten many Diet Cokes since that night.)

Then something happened and happened very quickly. Michael made a call, and we found ourselves sitting across the desks of Max Mutchnick and Dave Kohan, who had written a funny new pilot called *Will & Grace*, which was going to go to series. The day after our interview, I came home to my apartment from a catering gig in my thrift store tux—with the same tape holding the zipper closed—and there were two messages on the answering machine. The first was from a lawyer, whose name I got off a bus, telling me my bankruptcy had gone through, and the second telling me that Tracy and I had been hired to write on *Will & Grace*.

A reinvention was the perfect idea! Thank you, Madonna!

The show, as they say, was a hit. Which surprised people because Ellen DeGeneres's show, *Ellen*, had flamed out big. This was partly to do with the direction the show had taken and partly to do with the right wing coming for it hard. It seemed like a bad time to bring Gay back to TV. But the country was balls deep in the Bill Clinton/Monica Lewinsky story, so *Will & Grace* slipped in while the right wing was distracted.

We had the privilege to work with four of the funniest actors on TV, the best director, and one of the best writing rooms ever. Imposter syndrome, insecurity, fear—my old frenemies never left, but they receded into the background further and further with every idea, joke, and story we contributed.

I threw out my catering tux and bought another one for the Emmys, which I had made to look exactly like the '70s velvet one Warren Beatty wore in *Shampoo*. It had always been a dream of mine to have one. Was it also a dream of mine to sneak into Cher's dressing room and stare in awe at her wig, which had been flown in separately for her to wear on the show? Well, in that moment, it was.

Was it my dream to be the only one to see Madonna dancing to her own song backstage as she waited for the scene to start? It kind of was, but only after the fact.

Maybe dreams that you don't even know you had come true all the time and you don't even know it.

As the show went on, people would start to tell me that *Will & Grace* changed their lives. The writers got letters saying this from all over the country. Young Gay kids telling us they watched the show with their families, and it made them feel better about themselves. Even though the characters were made up, these kids felt less alone.

That's powerful. And more importantly, helpful for me.

When I met Chris, he told me that the show helped him come out to his family. They loved the show, and one day when he was home for a visit and was watching it with his parents, he suddenly said, "I'm Will. And after a beat, his mother said, Well, as long as you're not Jack," and they went back to enjoying the show together. Progress! With room for even more!

There was also hate mail. And hate messages on my answering machine. It never occurred to me to be "unlisted" in the phone book. I didn't even know I was in there until I got a handful of messages on my machine, one calling me a "fag" and wishing I would die of AIDS. I saved that one on my machine for a while, taking a kind of sick pride in it. I still have the material from JONAH—"Jews Offering New Alternatives To Homosexuality"—that was sent to my home. I appreciated a good acronym.

I'm so happy and grateful to have been a part of such a funny, groundbreaking show. Women would say to me, "I love that show!" And their boyfriends would say to me, "My girlfriend loves that show!" As the years went on, I started to hear, "My mother loved that show!" Which would eventually become, "My grandmother loved that show!" I'm proud to hear someone laughing at a rerun on a stairmaster at the gym. Am I, in some small way, responsible for people getting into better shape? I'd like to think so.

I wasn't raised with self-esteem but was fortunate enough to find a work-around—a job that people continually complimented me on. And they seemed to mean it! And some even hated me for it, which was almost as good.

Sometimes, you know you're good at something because people tell you you are. And the more they tell you, the more you keep doing it and—hopefully—the more they will tell you you're good at it. Again, math.

I no longer needed to redraw myself on my Etch A Sketch every day—I had other people do it for me!

It's not as good as being born with the gene for self-esteem, like Madonna was, but maybe it's the next best thing.

Spanking the Cat

I think I'm dating my cat. It occurred to me last night as I lay in bed trying to read a book, but was unable to because she kept pawing at it until I put it down and made room for her to lie on my chest. It's the perfect vantage point for her to stare adoringly into my face, something she loves to do when I get into bed every night. After she settled, she began to purr with such an intensity that in a human, it would be called hyperventilating. I was scratching behind her ears and whispering things to her that I know she likes, "You're so pretty! Yes, you are! You're the prettiest cat in Los Angeles, maybe even Beverly Hills! Everyone says so! Yes, they do!"

And as I cooed away all my resentment for not being able to read my book, I looked into her eyes and saw something more than simple contentment. Even something more than love. I saw intimacy. I was being intimate with my cat. And as if to confirm my thought, she leaned her head forward and gave me what I can only describe as a love bite, nipping my chin. She misjudged her strength, however, as sometimes happens in the throes of passion, and actually broke the skin and drew blood. This gave me pause to reflect on our relationship. There is decidedly something strange going on when you need a safe word with your cat.

Though I do believe she's in love with me, it would be a mistake to dismiss her as some sort of fag hag cat.[49] I think the fact that I'm Gay and she's a cat cancels out those negative stereotypes. Besides, she's not chubby.[50]

Each night, I hear her frantically race through the house from wherever she was napping to greet me at the door as I climb the stairs to the front porch. If she could, she'd be holding a dry martini for me and my ratty old house slippers. Then she rushes to her scratching pad, where I spank her until my hand starts to hurt. And she loves it. Really. I can't hit her hard enough. Or long enough. I'm the top, and she's the bossy bottom in our obscene nightly ritual. More than once, I've gone through this routine only to be reminded just how unsettling it is by the appalled look on a guest's face as I'm caught spanking my cat far longer and harder than society would deem decent.

I suspect she knows when I am leaving for a trip because on at least two occasions, she has thrown up in my suitcase. I believe if she could prevent me from going, she would, and I'd imagine an elaborate scheme of hers to do just that. I'd come home from work and slip on a pile of her cat toys, which she had cleverly spread all over the floor. I would fall and hit my head, only to awaken sometime later to find myself tied up with several of her long wire toys, the ones that look like an untwisted coat hanger with four or five cigarette buts at one end. After coming to my senses, I'd find her sitting a few feet away, staring at me and licking her feet like a thug cleaning his dirty nails with a switchblade. She'd slowly walk over and sniff.

---

49 I'm sorry, but I'm using this offensive term here.

50 Offensive again, but this time without an apology.

She might even dangle one of her fishing pole toys with the feathers on the end over my face out of anger or simply because she could.

Is it my fault? Are my compliments about how pretty she is somehow misconstrued as flirty? Is it something I put out? A neediness? After all, animals are very sensitive and can grow to resemble their owners not only outwardly but inwardly as well.

I had a dog, Mindy, who was forced to stay home with my parents after I left for college. She quickly took after my father and put on a lot of weight, lost a lot of fur, and eventually developed what sounded exactly like a smoker's cough. I remember a time when, coming home for spring break, she couldn't even be bothered to get her big bald ass off the couch to greet me. Instead, she sat watching stories with my mom, barely throwing me a look with an expression that seemed to say: *Be a doll and get me a fudgie from the freezer wouldya?*

I can place the blame for my current inter-species relationship squarely at the feet of my friend, Laura, a self-admitted crazy cat lady. She is the one who asked me to foster the cat for a few days after she rescued it from an abusive environment. Laura had people lined up who could come on Saturday and take her but needed a place for the cat to stay until then. Sophia was her name, but I didn't think it suited her. It seemed too classy. Sophia is a cat who is pampered and has lots of fluffy white hair and a pushed in nose.

This cat was the opposite of a Sophia, with a crooked tail, a rib that had been broken and healed badly so that it jutted out noticeably, and raging infections in both ears. She also came with the attitude of a gangbanger who was thrown off her roller derby team for aggressive behavior. Girl could scratch a bitch. For some reason, I renamed her Dr. Bellows after an *I Dream of*

Jeannie character, who also possessed an ambiguous sexuality.[51] That eventually got lengthened to Dr. Katherine Bellows and then to Dr. Katherine Louise Bellows and later shortened to just Kitty. It was easier to put on her stocking at Christmas. And less confusing at the vet.

I was surprisingly sad the following Saturday when a mother and her young daughter showed up to take her. I had started to become attached to my foster cat and was overjoyed to get the phone call the next day that the girl didn't like her new pet—would I please take her back? She was scared of her, the mom explained, and they were just going to buy a nice kitten at the mall instead. One with less attitude.

It took a full year of circling each other and giving her space before she came around and opened her heart to me. There were times when I felt like Elizabeth Taylor in *Cat on a Hot Tin Roof*, wearing a slip and screaming, "We don't live together! We occupy the same cage!"

I eventually won her over and came to love my little damaged furry companion. I bought her fresh tuna at the market and plastic tips for her nails, sometimes getting colored ones for holidays or just times when I thought we could use a little cheering up. We both benefitted. I fed her and she killed spiders for me. But more than that, she brought me out of my shell a little. And even though she was just a cat, she showed me an intimacy that I hadn't had for a long time. Not since the death of my boyfriend several years earlier.

Luis was diagnosed with leukemia in March 1992 and immediately began treatment. When he started to lose his hair, it was

[51] *I Dream of Jeannie* was a sitcom about a woman whose power was kept in check by her "master." And by the studio—she wasn't even allowed to show her belly button.

so gradual that we didn't notice for a while. We knew it would happen and we saw the hair on his pillow, but he had so much. Even his eyebrows thinned and the already meager triangle of hair on his chest eventually dwindled to nothing.

"Chemo head," he would call himself, and we joked that his superpowers were puking and crawling on the floor when his head hurt so bad he couldn't walk. I remember his parents coming from San Francisco to visit him during one of his hospital stays. Luis had asked me to bring the clippers from home—he wanted his head shaved so it wouldn't be so patchy. His father, feeling helpless, decided that the haircut was his job. And it was very hard to see this man, who up until that point had spent more time talking to the man in the next bed, shaving my beloved's head. Luis winced and tensed up, obviously in pain as his father roughly jabbed at him with the clippers, hair flying everywhere. It was my turn to feel helpless. He complained that it hurt, and his father snapped at him to be still, but Luis wouldn't have stopped him for anything.

Later, as I was spreading Keri lotion on some spots and bits of toilet paper on others, he asked me if I still thought he was cute. And I did.

Cats, of course, can't ask questions like that. They have their own way of communicating. Such as when Kitty peed on my pillow, and a pet psychic told me she merely wanted me to know that I was filling her litter box too high. Message received.

In some ways, I think Kitty prepared me to eventually welcome Chris into my life. Ironically, it was my friend Laura who introduced me to him as well. I believe she used the same tactic on me as before and promised I only had to foster him for a week and that a family would come for him, and would I just make sure he got two drops in his ears every morning? Like Kitty, I decided to keep him.

Not too long ago, a psychic—not the cat one, this one was more expensive—asked me out of the blue if we had someone's ashes in our bedroom. We did—we had a bit less than half. His parents had the other half of Luis. (Eventually I would regret that decision. I should've allowed his very Catholic, but loving, mother to have all of his ashes to bury. I just couldn't let go at that time.) This psychic told me true intimacy with Chris would never be achieved with them in the house. And since I want to believe my hundred and fifty bucks was well spent, we flew to San Francisco, where Luis was from, to finally spread them. I anticipated a problem at the Burbank airport but was pleasantly surprised to learn that in answer to the question of "What's in here?" all I had to say was "the ashes of my boyfriend—well, most of him"—and the screener waved me right through.

So off we went to spread Luis's ashes, and I have to say we had the best time.

Now, normally spreading your lover's ashes might not sound like a day at the beach. Unless the beach is where you're spreading them. I imagine that to most, it might seem like it should be accompanied by a good deal of crying. And I did cry a little, but mostly I was thinking: *What an asshole I must look like trying to throw ashes into the ocean when this shit just blows right back at you.* It's a romantic idea—the lone mourner standing on the rocks and returning their loved one to the sea from whence all came, but it's an idea that has been seen in countless films and TV shows. It's also a stupid one. The wind blows the wrong way, and it is a certainty that a lot of it will land in your hair and eyes and even in your mouth if you are dumb enough to have it open, which I did. I truly believe that not a speck of Luis went into the water. Most of him went on the rocks and on me and consequently in the plumbing at the fish and chips place along the highway where we stopped so I could clean up.

This has happened to me before, so you'd think I would have learned. That time, it wasn't at the ocean but at One Shubert Alley in Times Square. Before my friend Charles had died, he made it very clear that his ashes were to be spread on Shubert Alley and that his friends were to sing "I'll Be Seeing You." I guess he wanted to make goddamn sure there wouldn't be a dry eye there. Clearly, Charles was Drama. I saw him perform shortly before he died in a play his friend Jane had written. Though a great actor, it was hard to watch him struggle with his lines, his makeup barely concealing the KS lesions on his face.

We met there on a rainy and windy day—two prerequisites for ash-spreading—only to find Shubert Alley had been closed off with wooden barricades. We were informed by a security guard that it was closed once a year for cleaning, and this was the day. I imagine there is a lot of gum to scrape off left by various stalkers and Gay boys who did *A Chorus Line* in college and needed to make a pilgrimage to the holy site where it was originally performed (such as myself). They also needed to hose off the bum dung. This was Times Square of the early '90s, where hookers and crack whores roamed freely without worry that a family of German tourists in *Pirates of the Caribbean* T-shirts and Mickey Mouse ears might ruin their buzz.

This was also in the empowering days of AIDS activism, and we were not going to let a little barricade and an elderly security guard stand in the way of granting one of our comrade's final wishes. We had a higher calling. We knocked over the barricades and stormed the alley. Cops were summoned, but we didn't care. We threw our handfuls of ashes and sang

"I'll Be Seeing You" in voices choked with emotion. But still on key (well, I tried) because, after all, we did have an audience, and it was Shubert Alley, and our group was largely made up of theater queens of all genders. Afterwards, we went to brunch and took turns going to the restroom to wash Charles off our hands and faces. I don't think he would have minded since he loved brunch. I sometimes wonder how many ashes have entered the water supply in major cities this way.

Before my ill-advised trip to the sea, Chris and I spent a lovely day scattering Luis around sites in San Francisco where he and I had visited once many years ago on a trip to see his family, including various places in Golden Gate Park and a generous amount at the apartment building where *Tales of the City* was filmed.[52] Those books were his favorite. It took forever to find it, and we got some curious looks from some of the real people who actually lived there, but I know he'd be thrilled to rest, at least partially, at the spot where the worldly Trans woman, Mrs. Madrigal, met Mary Ann Singleton for the first time.

I felt I had taken intimacy to a whole other level. After all, what could be more intimate than spreading the ashes of your old boyfriend with your new one?

In 2010, Chris and I flew to the Galápagos Islands and took a tour of the Charles Darwin Research Station, where Lonesome George lived. Lonesome George was a ninety-year-old tortoise who was the last of his particular species. Apparently, before it was outlawed, tortoise hunting was a very popular sport and had eventually wiped out an entire population of them on the island of Pinta, except one lucky survivor who was found years

[52] *Tales of the City* are great books. They are written by Armistead Maupin. If you haven't already, read them immediately after this one. Then watch the TV adaptations—especially the first season, which is genius.

later: George. He was brought back to the Station and introduced to female after female in the hope of passing his genes along, but each time he ignored the female, never showing a desire for intimacy with any of them.

Momentarily forgetting I was in another country and seizing my inner ugly American, I said a little too loud, "Maybe he's Gay." All I got was some nervous laughter from the group and a dismissive answer from the guide along the lines of animal homosexual activity would be bred out of a species in order for it to survive. Sort of like Darwinian conversion therapy. But looking in George's eyes, I recognized something more than just a passing resemblance to Ian McKellen. There was something else. Something I recognized. A kind of kindred spirit. Someone who maybe just needed something to sit on his chest and bring him out of his shell.

That's why Chris and I are seriously thinking of sending Kitty to the Galapagos. What she and I have is just too weird.

How to Become Popular During an Epidemic

At some point in the 2000's, I was clicking through *The New York Times* online when I read something that gave me every feeling all at once. St. Vincent's Hospital in the Village was closing and was eventually going to be torn down. "Probably for NYU housing," I muttered to myself, alone in my kitchen. I find that I do that more and more these days. But it's better than muttering in front of others because that always results in a frustrated, "What?!" from the other person and then you have to say "Nothing," and they get weird and suddenly it's a thing that now exists.

This particular muttering was tinged with a bit of sadness and a weird kind of nostalgia. To a large group of people, St. Vincent's was "Ground Zero" for the AIDS-afflicted in NYC. At that time, it was synonymous with care for AIDS patients, particularly poor Gay men and drug users. Many protested it for its ties to Catholicism, historically not an ally of the Queer.

My friends and I referred to it as the "Death Star."

I used to spend a lot of time there, visiting Luis.

I didn't have many friends when I first moved to New York. I only ever had a few growing up (things changed briefly for a bit in college because drugs). I place a lot of the blame on my resting murder face. My mother always told me that as a baby, I never smiled. I frowned at birth and have continued ever since then. I used to tell her, "Well, I was waiting for something to make me smile." That made her feel bad, and, well, mission accomplished, I guess. All my life, strangers I'd pass on the street would say sweetly, "Smile!" as they passed. Some added "…it can't be that bad!" They all had good intentions, I suppose, but their comments made me frown even more, and today I spend a lot of money on products to erase all the lines they caused. One time, I was walking down a street in New York when I heard that familiar "Smile!" and I snapped back, "I can't! I was born without smile muscles!" There had been a segment on *20/20* or *60 Minutes* or one of those things about a girl who was born without smile muscles, and I never forgot the look on her face when someone told her a joke. She said it was funny, but it was like no one had told that to her face. If you were a stand-up you would never want her in the front row. Well, the person I snapped at was taken aback, but then she looked at me with sympathy. Had she seen the show too?

I started going to ACT UP meetings in the late '80s because I wanted to do what I could about the AIDS epidemic, which politicians seemed to not give a shit about.[53] And maybe meet

[53] ACT UP—AIDS Coalition to Unleash Power—is an international grassroots political group working to end the AIDS crisis and improve the lives of people living with HIV and AIDS through direct action, medical research, treatment, and advocacy. The meetings were also great places to get yourself some activist D.

some people. Which wasn't easy because I would sit in the back, nervous about talking to anyone. I felt the way I've always felt when not high—like I didn't quite fit in. Of course, I wore the uniform: black Dr. Martens, tight jean cutoffs that went to the knee, and a T-shirt of my choosing. Mine was almost always a white tank top with some sort of royal symbol of some sort of country with some sort of meaning to it.

And I would join in the marches and protests alone, knowing it was important I was there, but still feeling self-conscious and awkward. I'd infiltrate various groups and join in their chants, but I couldn't shake the feeling that I was intruding. And even though I'm sure it was not the case, it felt like as soon as I joined in on the chant, it would trail off, and I would be forced to slink away to join another group and destroy their chant.

Was it my fault? Did I disrupt the flow somehow? Did someone from that group hear me accidentally chant, "A PEOPLE UNITED WILL NEVER BE DEFEATED!," realizing too late that the word is "divided," not "defeated?" Which makes more sense because it rhymes?

My favorite chant of the time was the one we all turned to as the hours dragged on, "NO MORE CHANTING!! NO MORE CHANTING!!" This only caused confusion to those bystanders looking on, but fun to do and fun to see the occasional pedestrian get it.

When I got a boyfriend, I would march with him and his friends, though they were a bit showier than I would prefer, dancing in choreo'd routines. It actually made it so much worse for me. I couldn't master how to chant, dance, and march at the same time. Gays can often make things difficult.

It was announced that there was going to be a demo at the CDC—the Center for Disease Control—in Atlanta. And

I was excited to go for many reasons: It was important, my ticket was bought for me by an ACT UP fund, I was going with my boyfriend at the time, and I had just gotten this super cool black leather jacket that I bought for almost nothing at a Salvation Army. (This was before we knew how homophobic that particular organization was. Or maybe I knew but was ignoring it because it was a super cool black leather jacket for almost nothing.)

The guy who I was dating at the time was mean to me, often criticizing my body. And I rationalized it by thinking: *Maybe he's right!* After all, I thought the same things and maybe it's just good to have confirmation! I think it was also the fact that he was my first boyfriend. I didn't know the rules yet. Like: He's supposed to be nice. He once told me that he could tell I would be fat when I got older. Coming from a family with that particular gene, it was something I worried about too, and it made me think: *He knows me!*

His final act of mean was to break up with me right before the trip to Atlanta. I was heartbroken. And I had to scramble for a reassignment to a different room in the shitty motel we were staying at.

The new room had two big beds in it, and I suddenly had to share a bathroom with three Gay guys I didn't know and share a bed with one of them. Two guys named Luis and Juan shared one, and a guy named Ricardo and I shared the other. Apparently, a member of the Latina/o Caucus had cancelled at the last minute, so they had half a bed for this sad anxious white guy.

Being Gay and sharing a bed with a Gay stranger, we naturally started fooling around. Well, I don't know if it was my innate anxiety or the fact that Luis and Juan were asleep—or more likely, pretending to sleep—a few feet away, but things were over for me very quickly. Embarrassment. Humiliation. Now not only did I have to march at the CDC with a huge group of people I didn't know, I had to avoid the one I did.

The next day, we protested at the CDC, and it was pissing down rain. It seemed to rain harder than it had ever rained in history, and it was difficult not to take it personally. I spent my time walking in a circle, chanting till my throat was sore and trying not to freak out about my super cute new black leather jacket. How much rain could it withstand?

On the plane home, I had to put my super cute new black leather jacket in a plastic garbage bag because it just would not dry. It was destroyed, but I wasn't ready to let go just yet.

Back in New York, Luis, from the other bed at the shitty motel, asked for my number at the next meeting. He was cute and sweet, but I had the brief thought that Ricardo had spread the word about me and everyone knew what had happened in that bed in that shitty motel. Was Luis going to lure me into sitting closer to the front at the next meeting and then, when the moment was right, signal the room and everyone would laugh at me and point and throw condoms? I don't know why it would be condoms, but they had to throw something, didn't they?

Well, I never got to live out that *Carrie-esque* fantasy. I was relieved but also not—I was weirdly looking forward to it.

Luis and I dated, and his many friends became my friends, and my few friends became his, especially Tracy. He was the opposite of me—open, free-spirited, unselfconscious, and happy, happy, happy. Always smiling. He smiled for both of us. The thing I muttered the most those days was, "What the fuck does he see in me?"

And his smile was infectious. It eventually caused me to smile more.

One day, a surly stranger I passed on the street said, "What's so fuckin' funny?" That made me smile even more.

And he knew what he wanted. After several months he gave me an ultimatum: We move in together or break up. Like so many Gays, he was drama. And even though he had this huge, amazing poster of Madonna from *Truth or Dare* and I immediately knew where it would hang in my apartment, I was caught off guard. But before I had to make such a life altering decision, he got cancer, and the decision was more or less made for me. We moved him into my place so he could take care of me. I mean so *I* could take care of *him*. But really, I mean so he could take care of me.

And he did. He was so good at being sick and I was so bad at him being sick. We were the perfect couple!

When he periodically had to check into the hospital, he had so many visitors that he was constantly violating the "maximum number of visitors" rule. If the nurses felt like counting, they would see he had fifty "close family members."

At St. Vincent's, I not only spent as much time as I could with Luis, I also—if they were up to it—visited people in the AIDS ward. I became so familiar with that main entrance, I used to say a quiet "Hi" to the plaque of Dr. William Francis Norman O'Loughlin, who was one of the attending physicians on the Titanic. It made sense to me that he greeted survivors of another disaster. And many, like himself, who didn't survive.

The nurses weren't always friendly, but if you were lucky, you got Frida, who gave out more passes than were allowed, and sometimes even after visiting hours were over.

I would bring her a donut on my visits, and I would bring Luis one of the macrobiotic meals served at the Manhattan Center for Living on lower Broadway which helped provide meals and other services for people afflicted with AIDS and HIV. I'm sure it's overpriced NYU housing now. Or an over-priced Lululemon, where the over-priced students shop. The Center would prepare a bag lunch for me, and I would deliver it to him, and then I'd eat his hospital food while he ate the good, healthy stuff.

There was always a constant stream of visitors, many from ACT UP. Luis had many friends. And I felt like I was getting some of the runoff just by being near him. He was the shark, and I was the remora—the fish that swims under the shark getting the food that falls out of its mouth.

Sometimes, when I came in with his lunch, Luis's doctor would be there taking him through a guided meditation. I would quietly eat his Jell-O and read one of his books such as *You Can Heal Your Life* by the self-help guru Louise Hay. Louise believed AIDS was a message from the body, "the final attempt of one's own consciousness to communicate." Cancer was caused by resentment, and the cure was forgiveness. I remember wanting to scream, "Fuck you, Louise Hay!" but stopping myself just in case there was something to that shit.

It all came down to self-love. People believed this stuff at the time. And I pretended to. I still pretend to, that's how powerful it is.

I spent a lot of time at St Vincent's, squeezing in next to Luis, just talking or sometimes fooling around. The nurses learned to announce themselves louder than usual, but I'm sure we weren't the only room in that place where they had to do that. There wasn't enough space on the walls for all the cards he got, so I spent a lot of time decoupaging his room. And throwing out dead flowers and bringing overflow to other rooms. Someone brought him a blow-up version of Munch's *The Scream*, which he loved.

I remember laying in his bed watching the Oscars with him and hoping that Jodie Foster would win for *Silence of the Lambs*, a movie that was very good, but very homophobic. It seemed to me to have at least ten different Gay serial killers in it. I remember the scene where the main killer revealed he had a pierced nipple, and the audience screamed. It was basically a jump scare. We were hoping Jodie would use the opportunity to come out. Well, she won, but she didn't say anything about being Gay. We heard a lot of boos on the AIDS ward below us that night.

Luis was in and out of the hospital that summer and fall. The last time he went in, he went directly to the ICU. And he didn't come back out. It was a horrible, horrible night. I woke up drenched in his sweat and when I took his temperature, it was so high that to this day, I don't let myself think of the number. He had shit himself and couldn't walk, and there were other awful things that I can't remember or don't let myself remember. I do remember the ambulance, and the next thing I remember is coming back to get a few things that were needed and to try to wash the shit out of his underwear. I don't know why I didn't just throw them away, but it seemed important at the time.

I got to know the waiting area outside the ICU very well. It became another home away from home. And, of course, I was never alone.

There was always someone to ask me how I was doing—did I need anything? At first, I always said "No thanks, I'm fine." I didn't want to be a nuisance. But eventually I started saying "Yes." "Maybe just a coffee from the machine?" Then: "Maybe a donut?" "How 'bout a magazine?" Then: "Hmm, maybe that better coffee across the street. And not just a shitty donut from the cafeteria, what about a Krispy Kreme? But no—" I would hastily add—"that's too far! It's all the way over on Twenty-Third!"

"Oh, I don't mind," they would say, and off they would go to do my bidding.

But for the most part, when I couldn't be in his room, I would sit in the waiting area just outside the ICU, with Tracy in those horrible rounded plastic chairs, in a daze. People patted me. I discovered I liked being patted. And I didn't have to entertain. I didn't have to give them a reason to want to be around me—to not run away from them before they realized how undeserving I was of their attention. I didn't have to do anything. They came to me. What was this unfamiliar feeling?

Most of my memories are very hazy during that time. It seemed like weeks, but...well, maybe it was, who knows now? Maybe Dr. William Francis Norman O'Loughlin does. Hopefully, his plaque is somewhere prominent now and not in a dollar bin at a Salvation Army.

I remember smoking in the stairwell just down the hall from the ICU. I didn't even smoke, but it was my way of saying, "I'm grieving, I do whatever the fuck I want!" I remember Miss Coco, my drag queen friend, holding me as I entered a particularly prolonged sobbing session. No one can soothe like a drag queen.

I remember asking my friend Roger to call his mother—who did the voice of Wilma Flintstone—and have her talk to Luis as Wilma, even though he was in an induced coma, and we never really knew how aware he was. My friend John sang one of Luis's favorite songs, "Day By Day" from *Godspell.* Which isn't the best song because if you're not careful, it could go on forever. I remember him singing quietly into Luis's ear while we smiled and watched. Eventually, his face started to show some strain, so a few of us picked up the tune with him, also singing quietly. But how long can a group of Gays keep a song quiet—especially when no one seems to be able to bring it to some sort of satisfying conclusion? Well, the nurses did that when they came in and asked us to shut the fuck up and get our asses back to the waiting room. And why were there so many of us in his room anyway? There were rules, etc....

But rules didn't really matter then. Everyone who tried to enforce them was the enemy, especially to the members of ACT UP who seemed to be taking over the waiting room outside the ICU in alarming numbers, leaving little room for other grieving family members visiting their own loved ones. Something had to be done, and the head nurse, or head someone, came and demanded that everyone except two people had to leave. Well, no. It quickly got heated, and Bob Rafsky—who famously cockblocked President Clinton when he was working his way through a crowd, and demanded to know what he was doing for AIDS and AIDS research—got indignant and loud. Normally, I loved a confrontation, a chance to vent my anger, but I was not up for it that day. Thankfully some level-headed Queers diffused the situation and most of the visitors left. For a bit.

I remember seeing Luis for that last time. I was alone with him and telling him how much I loved him, and he had a moment. It's a moment that I do not allow myself to think about. I don't really even remember it, but at the same time, I will never forget it.

On the night he died, I went to usher for a play. Luis and I had made plans to do it weeks before because we wanted to see *The Night Larry Kramer Kissed Me*, and it was a way to do it for free. Everyone thought I should be surrounded by friends that night, but I decided that doing what Luis and I were going to do would be the right thing. And I knew I was right when, after helping people to their seats, I felt my face tingle. It started as a gentle tingle but got more and more intense for several minutes before fading away. He was there. I knew it. And he had found a way to let me know that. And to see the play with me without having to do the work of showing people to their seats.

From that point, my memories become even more blurry and out of order. At some point, Luis was cremated. His very Catholic parents were opposed to that but went along with it because those were his wishes. I recall a funeral in a church, which we agreed to do for them. As I was speaking and saying whatever I said, I had the thought that Luis would be rolling over in his urn if he was watching this, and I had to suppress a laugh. It wasn't really even an urn, it was still the plastic container that the funeral home provided, covered in pink triangle stickers.[54]

That night at my apartment—or maybe it was another night—we had a gathering of our closest friends. We played Bronski Beat, The Smiths, Gipsy Kings, all of his favorite

[54] The Pink triangle was what Nazis made Homosexuals and Trans women wear in the camps to distinguish them from the others. In the '70s it was revived, turned upside down (the triangle pointing upright), and used as a symbol of protest and pride. Fun fact: It's an emoji now.

music.[55] We made an altar with the box of ashes in the middle and surrounded it with things he loved—pictures, political buttons, his favorite rainbow triangle necklace, food he loved... His parents were there, his father looking particularly uncomfortable, out of his element. He came to life when my friend Steve stopped by, kneeled at the altar, said a prayer, and then crossed himself. I remember how his father's face changed from confused and uncomfortable to relieved.

For the first time in my life, I understood how Catholicism could be used for good. It gave his parents faith, which somehow made them strong enough to endure one of the worst things imaginable—the death of a child. I forgave the religion I was raised in just the tiniest bit.

Later that night, when we watched Luis's performance as Linda Ronstadt, his father proudly shouted, "He looks just like Linda!" He didn't, but it was nice that his dad was so excited by that thought. Of course, this being New York, we had a mean downstairs neighbor, and of course she came to complain about the noise. "It sounds like you have a dozen people in there all walking around in high heels!" Well, I don't know if it was a dozen, but there were more than a few. Later, when I'd pass her on the stairs, I'd feel like an asshole, but that night, it was empowering to sweep open the door and loudly exclaim: "My lover just died! Do you think, for tonight, we might make a little noise?!" She slunk away. It was drama and I needed a bit.

That all happened in November. My birthday was coming up in a week. I never really made a big fuss out of my birthday, and needless to say, that year I wasn't planning to make a fuss at all. I would have sat alone in my apartment or maybe gotten a

[55] This was long before the world learned what a racist asshole Morrissey is.

bite to eat with Tracy, but someone—I don't remember who—asked if they could take us out. I don't remember if anyone yelled "Surprise!" but there ended up being a table of ten or twelve people, mostly Luis's friends that I had gotten to know fairly well during those agonizing weeks. They were having a birthday party for me! I think maybe my first one ever!

I remember my new friend, Rachel, got me a cactus. My first present at my first party. And it was a living thing!

I had friends! Many friends! For the first time in my life, I was popular! And all it took was unfathomable loss!

In life, it's important to find your tribe. Death helped me find mine.

People continued to check in, asking if I would like to get a cup of coffee or a bite to eat at Stingy Lulu's, a cheap diner with drag queen waitresses. I actually found myself turning down plans—that was a new thing for me.

Even the homophobic chef at the restaurant where I worked—who only spoke to the women—said "Sorry about your friend." I think those who lost a lover got that expression a lot. After a while, I stopped correcting it.

Even in death, Luis forced me to stay in contact with people. He had left me a will—well, a list on the back of a "Lesbian Avengers" handout—of things he wanted important people in his life to have after he passed. It was a long list: The Madonna poster to Sam (goddammit, it was perfect on my wall!); his Pee Wee Herman watch to his friend, Alfredo. The list went on and on. He wanted his doctor to have his plastic blow up version of Munch's *The Scream*. I wasn't sure if his patients would appreciate seeing this in the waiting room of his office, but on the other hand, Queers are not the type to shy away from gallows humor.

The only person on the list I couldn't get Luis's gift to was his nephew, Armando, who was only four or five at the time. Luis wanted him to have some Gay comic books he had collected. They followed the life of "ordinary" Queer people—I think they were called *Tales of the Closet*. It wasn't that he thought his young nephew was Gay; Luis wanted Armando to have them because, to him, they represented forward movement in the fight for Gay rights. He felt they were important, and he wanted to leave them to someone special. But when I called his mother, she said that maybe I should hold onto them for a while since Armando was so young.

I am still close to some of the friends I made at that time. Some faded away only to resurface as Facebook friends. Some died. I was able to memorialize one of Luis's closest friends, Juan, in a line on *Will & Grace*. Jack has stolen a gym card, and Grace looks at it and says, "Poor Juan Mendez, sitting at home, his ass dimpling." Standards and practices allowed that because there were many, many Juan Mendez's who lived in New York. But I'd like to think that wherever Juan was, he knew it was him being referred to. Or, if he didn't catch it the first time, maybe he found out during syndication, and it made him smile.

I recently got in touch with Luis's nephew, Armando, on Facebook. It was his uncle's birthday, and I decided to message him. I wasn't sure if he'd respond or remember me or if he'd even care. But he did respond, and he called me, and we spoke for a long time. He was happy to hear me tell stories of his Uncle Luis. I sent him photos of Luis and I—some with him and his sister eating sandwiches in Muir Woods, where we took them on a hike. I even sent him the drawings he made for Luis and I the first time we visited his family in San Francisco. He was three years old, and I remember a particularly horrible moment when he came in to wrestle with Luis and I, and Luis's father freaked out, pulling Armando off us and out of the room with a horrified look on his face. The art he made for us shortly after helped smooth the edges off that hideous memory. I was happy I could finally cross the last name off the list that Luis had made for me. I sent Armando the comic books. I even sent them in the ratty manila envelope that they had sat in for thirty years, on which Luis had written "For Armando, with love, Uncle Luis." We still message each other once in a while.

Chris and I eventually had Luis's name added to the AIDS Memorial Grove in Golden Gate Park in San Francisco. He would be honored to be there.

Armando told me where Luis was buried, and Chris and I went to his grave at the Mt. Olivet Cemetery in Colma, CA. But strangely, they didn't have a record of him. After much searching, we discovered he didn't really have a grave. His ashes had just been buried between his parents with no marker. I could only assume that was a thing in the Catholic Church—you can't bury half a person. Maybe god gets confused easily. After all, They weren't as young as They once were. I left some ACT UP buttons on the dirt where I thought he would be. I knew he'd like that.

Well, they tore down most of St Vincent's. Some of the hospital buildings were converted into luxury condos, and a new luxury building, Greenwich Lane, replaced the St. Vincent's building. Rich people live, eat, and work out in a fancy gym where many suffered and many died. I hope they never saged it. I hope their fancy gym is haunted by Gay ghosts who, after their Gay ghost workout, do some damage. Maybe they turn up the speed on the treadmills, causing the tenants to crash onto the gym floor, break a bone, and need a hospital. That thought makes me smile.

Sweating With Lesbians

"*Es un buen día para morir.*" It's a good day to die. I overheard someone say this as I made my way to yoga. Chris and I were on vacation at a Queer yoga retreat. Though we didn't do much yoga—we mostly retreated from it.

"It's a good day to die." At first, it sounds like a morbid thing to say, but when you think about it, it's actually positive. If it's a "good day," maybe that means everything is right and in order and you are happy—maybe the happiest you've ever been. And in that case, wouldn't it be a good time to exit? To leave the party when it's still going on, as it were? An Irish or French exit—I've heard both. You don't want to be one of those party guests who wears out their welcome. The ones who drink too much and get sloppy. We've all seen—or been—them. They get loud and slur stories about famous people they "know."

And they trash those poor celebs. They always do. "I heard Anne Hathaway is a bitch!" They claim they have a friend who worked on a set, and she got Starbucks for everyone except the *one extra*! Well, maybe that one extra was an asshole. "I heard Emmy Rossum likes to get peed on." This is a good one, and

I think I've used it myself at parties, pulling it out when there was a lull in the conversation and I was worried the person I was talking to would get bored of me. Sorry, Emmy. But in my defense, I did hear that from someone, somewhere. Probably at a party.

These were the thoughts going through my head as I laid on the floor in the fetal position in a sweat lodge in Tulum, Mexico, on Christmas Day. I was feeling that combination of things where you want to be open to all experiences and at the same time think it's dumb as fuck. I tried not to giggle as our guides—two tattooed, fierce Lesbians with yoga bodies and twelve earrings in each ear—took us through a "rebirth." Even though I couldn't entirely wipe the smirk from my face, I was enjoying the darkness. I could barely see the red light from the hot rocks reflected off their toe rings. Before the door closed, they asked each of us to speak to the group, which horrified me. The only thing I hate more than speaking to a group is spiders. Speaking to a group of spiders would cause me to seize up and go unconscious like a fainting goat.

I was sitting to the immediate right of one of the sisters and was asked to speak first. Unfortunately, I wasn't paying attention when she said what to speak about. I'm sure it was some bullshit like "What do you want to get out of this?" Or "What do you want for the world?" But I panicked, and since I was the only guy, I took the easy way out. "I'm honored to be among these women. I believe that the future is female." I said that. I did. And even though I sort of meant it, I felt eyes rolling and some of them thinking, "Oh my god this asshole thinks he's woke or whatever."

One of the women talked about the universe. "It's like the universe was telling me to leave one of my wives and, I don't know, become one of my own wives." Oh. Maybe that was what we were supposed to talk about—the universe. Christ, I hope not. That concept has always confused me. Is the universe something to pray to? Something you just trust implicitly? Is it a place? You know how your grandma watches you as you masturbate? I think the universe is watching her watch you and shaking its head at the whole ugly scene. It also seems like the universe has a lot of places to watch over. Is it stretched too thin? Is it tired?

They say it gives you signs.

The woman who left one of her wives had found a lingerie model and took that to mean replacing the one wife with the model meant she could finally have the *model* family she always wanted. To her, it was a sign. I can get behind signs. Especially if they're literal. I knew I had to lose weight when I saw my mother's refrigerator magnet that read: "EAT, DRINK, AND BE MERRY FOR TOMORROW YOU DIET!" Which, now that I was thinking about it, might be what that person was saying—"a good day to diet." Maybe I'd misheard. Do "die" and "diet" sound the same in Spanish? I was also beginning to think I'd sweated too much and might pass out. Would the universe step in to help or just sit back and see how it played out?

The door was officially closed, and we were plunged into inky blackness, the only light coming from the steaming red rocks reflected in the aforementioned toe rings. I was thankful. It was nice to be hidden, sitting alone with my thoughts and trying not to fart. Which is something to be grateful for because otherwise, this small group of women would've been hotboxing gas from the "Nachos with the works!" that I'd had earlier. It was kind of peaceful and the herbs I'd rubbed on myself were nice. And the farts I no longer chose to hold in were made undetectable by the myriad smells evolving as our journey went on. I remember thinking a lot about Luis, my first lover. Lover. Cringe. Makes him sound like he was a piece on the side.[56] Luis had been dead for many years at that point.

I wondered what he would think of me now. He used to sit behind me with his arms around me, feel my stomach, and affectionately call me "Buddha Belly." In that sweat lodge I was imagining him doing the same thing but with genuine concern for my health.

I used to believe. In god. Then this "universe" idea. I used to have faith, but by the time I arrived in New York at the end of the '80s, I didn't see how anyone possibly could. By then, AIDS had taken hundreds of thousands of lives, a large majority of them Gay men. The parade of Gays carrying signs with my image on them and singing, "Willkommen, bienvenue, welcome!" as I stepped off the bus, was not going to materialize. New York was not going to be all about me and my dreams.

I did what I could with the rest of the Queers—marching, chanting, yelling, blocking traffic, getting arrested. I learned to love ecstasy because it helped simulate happiness for a while, staved off the anger for a bit. And even though Luis's cancer was not HIV-related, the grief of his death was added to the already steaming red-hot ball of rage that fueled me through that time. Why would the universe allow this? Why would it kill so many Gay men, many of them who should've had a whole lifetime ahead of them? Time to be creative, fall in love, get heartbroken, have great sex, have bad sex. All my yet-to-be-identified ex-boyfriends, tricks, two-night stands, fuck buddies?

---

[56] We used to call our significant others "lovers." I hated it but I did it. I also hate "significant others."

All the jerks whose rejection of me would've supposedly made me stronger?

They should not have died horrible, premature deaths, many of them rejected by their families. Was it preordained that my generation would have to watch so many of their friends die? How did that make sense? Was the universe a Mean Girl? If so, then the universe was a little bitch that needed to be wrestled to the ground before it did any more damage.

There couldn't possibly be a plan or a logic to what was happening—one that we couldn't know about but simply had to trust.

Sometimes, I think about the tsunami in Indonesia in 2004 that killed over 200,000 people. There was a man on the news who was rescued after he was found clinging to a floating tree. He said he prayed to god to be saved, and god answered his prayers. I remember thinking: *Why you?* I'm sure everyone there prayed to god to be saved, so why did god pick this guy over 200,000 other people? Because somehow he was better than all them? And do trees even float? I don't know. It must've been a special kind of floating tree. Maybe god invented it just for him.

So, no—I didn't believe in god or the universe.

As I was having these thoughts all curled up like a farting baby, it occurred to me: I was so hot that it might be the day I actually did die. And it was too early in the day to know if it was a good one or not. I hadn't even had the first of my two naps.

Then one of the sisters must have seen—with her expert Lesbian night vision—that I was ready to go into the light, and she leaned in very close and whispered into my ear, "We got you." She tilted a bottle of water to my mouth, and I had an image of myself as a helpless baby bird. And I was soothed. Then she opened the door a crack to let in a little air, poured more water on the rocks, said a few things about strength and how important it was to take care of ourselves and others, and I started to cry.

And I realized what I do believe in. It's not the universe. I believe in Lesbians.

When I think about what helped guide us all through that awful time, I think of Lesbians.

In many ways, they were the caretakers of the AIDS epidemic. When Doctors, scientists, and politicians refused to give a shit, Lesbians stepped up. They worked side by side with Gay men and helped keep us strong, mentally and physically. They gave us hope and reminded us of the importance of a unified community. This strength seemed to be in their genes, like the lioness, who hunts for food and won't let the deadbeat dad lion near the kids.

They know shit. And they get that shit done. Even while dealing with a government that refused to see how HIV/AIDS directly affected them as well as men. For some reason, their no-nonsense approach seemed to work better than my semi-nonsense approach.

A Lesbian would have talked sense into the floating tree guy. She wouldn't have allowed that tsunami to happen in the first place. Maybe that's too far. Maybe I'm putting them on a pedestal—but they built the goddamn pedestal, shouldn't they be allowed to stand on it?

One summer, I was the volunteer coordinator at Columbia Hospital and was tasked with organizing the Christmas gathering for women with HIV and their children, many of whom were positive as well. My Drag Queen friends were great at face painting, but it was Dykes on Bikes who pulled up in front on their motorcycles with tons of food they collected from various catering events around town.[57] All organized by my friend Heidi.

The Christmas Eve after Luis died, my friends and I had drinks at Dick's Bar, which was on the corner of Second Avenue and Twelfth Street. This would become a tradition I looked forward to, but that night, I just needed to be with people more than anything. And that skanky bar was perfect. What Skanky bar isn't? My friend Charlie played "C30 C60 C90 Go!" by Bow Wow Wow on the jukebox over and over, pissing off all the queens who had put their money in to play Mariah Carey's "All I Want For Christmas is You" over and over. There was even food laid out on the pool table that you didn't dare touch until you'd had too many margaritas to care. The buffet was surrounded by a string of old-timey Christmas lights, half the bulbs broken or missing.

Later that night, Heidi and her girlfriend walked me down Thirteenth Street to my apartment. There was never a lot of foot traffic on that street, so hundreds of rats would always scatter away from you as you proceeded down it. And there were always a few that didn't scatter, that stared you down. I think that night some wore Santa Claus hats. At my door, they stopped me and asked, again, if I wanted to stay over at their place for the night. They knew it would be hard for me to be alone. I said no, I could take care of myself. I was a proud, Gay man—out, loud, and drunk!

[57] Dykes on Bikes, started in 1976, is a chartered Lesbian motorcycle club. They're fierce. They have a 501(c)(3) nonprofit status, which seems cool. Back in the day, the word "Dyke" was used freely by the Queer community. Like other slurs, it had been reclaimed and made empowering by the group it was originally meant to denigrate. It seems to have fallen out of favor with the younger Queers. I miss it. I also miss "Miss Thing." And obviously "fag hag."

Then I called them at three in the morning sobbing so loud it sounded fake. If it was a movie, that scene would be the one *I* knew would get me an Oscar but would actually get me roundly trounced by the critics. Maybe even earn me a Razzie nom. Heidi and her girlfriend came and got me and set me up nice and comfy on their futon couch and then went back to their futon bed. I was soothed. And comfortable—they had surprisingly expensive sheets. As she turned out the light, Heidi whispered into my ear, "You can do this—you're stronger than you think." This was from a woman who got ritual scarring on her arms, so I had no other option than to make her words come true.

When the door to the sweat lodge finally opened wide, letting the Mexican sun in, I didn't feel like I had any answers, but I was feeling better than when we started. Who gets answers anyway? I got something better—I felt taken care of. Did I feel reborn? I don't know. Since I don't remember what it was like to be born in the first place, how would I know what it was like to do it again? I knew that I felt such an appreciation for those two funky sisters. I think I even smiled to myself—always a creepy thing to do.

When we were outside and finishing our complimentary coconut water and papaya, I called out: "Happy holidays!" and walked back to my hut. One of the women called after me: "Thank you for bringing your male energy!"

Were they mocking me? I thought I saw their eyes roll past me on the freshly raked path. But I didn't care if they were. They had a right to! I had Big Asshole Energy going into that sweatbox. But not coming out. I felt lighter. And I felt I deserved the fishbowl margarita that Chris and I shared, even though we were told over and over to make sure we drink tons of water and under no circumstances have alcohol. Maybe that's why I had severe diarrhea later that night.

The rest of that day, I found myself in a very light-hearted mood. The sisters had restored my faith in the universe. But I had questions for it: Does the universe want to help me? Is it too late? Will it forgive me or hold a grudge? What if it just doesn't like me? Maybe I said or did something that bugged it. Like maybe it loves Emmy Rossum and Anne Hathaway and thinks I'm a dick for repeating those things.

One time at a party, I trashed Jane Fonda for no reason, and a woman who overheard came up to me and said, "I know Jane Fonda, and she is an angel. How dare you trash her!"

And, of course, I doubled down since what else could I do? "Well, maybe I know a bit more about her than you do!" I said and stormed off. When in doubt, always act indignant. Maybe someday people will be trashing you at parties and then you'll know you've arrived.

It's comforting to know when I die and meet the universe—if that's even something that happens—I know it's going to be a fierce Lesbian. Maybe even all of them, rolled up into one giant person. With a dash of Annette Bening because you always need her. She will be sitting on a comfy chair with small Gay guys scurrying at her feet. They are in togas for some reason. And I will smile my creepy smile and feel taken care of.

The Ghosts of Harvey and Marilyn

"Do you, Jon, take Chris to be your spouse and to live together as partners, to treat him with love and respect, and to build a marriage that grows stronger and more loving as time passes?" the smiling Lesbian clerk at San Francisco City Hall asked.

"Um, yes?"

It was 2008, and same sex marriage had just been made legal in California. But soon, we expected, to be made illegal again when Prop 8—a California ballot proposition and a state constitutional amendment intended to ban same-sex marriage—would pass that fall and our asshole Governor Schwarzenegger would sign it into law. Chris wanted to get married because it was romantic, and I agreed to it, but only to swell the numbers and make a statement—that seemed much more important. It was activism, I told myself (and, as a bonus, it was Chris's birthday, and I told him marriage was his present that year).

It helped me to know that we stood where Marilyn Monroe and Joe DiMaggio did when they got married. Or at least that's what the exuberant clerk told us. We asked the couple who had just gotten married before us—a Gay couple who flew in from Florida with their dog, all in matching sweaters—if they would be our witnesses and they were more than happy to. They beamed at us, seeing a loving couple making their dream come true. Everyone there was happy, happy, happy for us and for what we were doing. I felt kind of guilty as I sipped my Starbucks frozen macchiato—extra shot of espresso, one pump of chocolate.

I didn't want to get married. When Chris first brought it up, the activist in me said "no." I was against all of that heteronormative bullshit. I felt the LGBT community (we had less letters then) had more important issues than getting married or serving openly in the military (or donating blood, that one was just because I hated needles). Marriage, military, and blood. I was happy that I couldn't do any of that. And now I was required to do all three. We want what they have, we want our place at the table. That was the argument. But if we had to sit at any table, I was happy not to be at the one with all the heterosexuals. You know it's not going to be the fun one.

I hated the idea of marriage even as a kid. My parents didn't exactly provide good marital role models. They never once in my childhood really acknowledged each other, except when my mother would complain about my father. "Sits on his ass all day! The roof needs fixing, the house needs painting, the grass needs roofing, the trees need painting, the paint needs roofing…!" I heard it all so much that it blurred together and just became words of complaint.

To me, they seemed unhappy and mismatched, and I was sure it was my fault somehow. But it wasn't like I asked them to have me. They definitely weren't pro-choice—I had not been consulted as to whether I even *wanted* to be born. I spent a lot of time under my desk wishing they would get a divorce. Even my "acceptable" boy dolls that I played with didn't get married, they started out that way and went through long, acrimonious divorces. G.I. Joe got all the weapons, and Big Jim got the jeep.[58]

"I'm not getting married," I would say as a kid when talk of my future would come up. The adults would laugh, "You'll want to when you meet the right girl." They never even considered that the right girl would be a boy.

Of course, if I absolutely *had* to be married, I would become the grieving young widower. There was drama and power in that role. But if she had to survive, I had a backup plan. I would marry Barbara Eden from *I Dream of Jeannie*. We would live in her bottle. I wasn't sure where we'd poop, but I figured since she was a genie, she'd be the one to work it out.

It wasn't that I didn't love Chris. I did. And it seemed kind of destined to be. We had been fixed up by two different people at the same time on opposite coasts. Our mutual friend, Laura, who worked with me on *Will & Grace*, told each of us separately that she knew someone we should meet. Meanwhile in New York, another mutual friend, Blair, told each of us separately that he knew someone we should meet. Laura and Blair did not know each other. Meant to be? I don't know if I believed that, but an accidental meeting in a Gay bar—remember those?—in

[58] Big Jim was a G.I. Joe–type action figure. He was hotter than Joe, who had a threatening, hardened look to him. You got the feeling his PTSD could cause him to snap at any moment. If you pressed the button on Jim's back, he karate chopped, and when you bent his arm, his bicep bulged. The downside is he set up unrealistic expectations for me in what a doll should look like.

Silver Lake when Chris was in LA for a job thing, seemed to cement the idea that it might be.

I simply thought there were more important fights to be had. For instance, legal protections. The right to visit your loved ones in hospitals or prisons—places reserved for "family members only." The right to not be thrown out of apartments, fired from jobs, or have your kids taken away because you're a same sex couple. Important shit like that. This didn't include certain hetero-imitatative behaviors such as the right to throw a bouquet of flowers to desperate, grasping singles in a banquet hall. Or the right to be Gay groomzillas or Lesbian bridezillas, screaming, "I said 'no baby's breath in the goddamn flower arrangements!' Will someone please get the *goddamn* baby's breath out of my sight! Jesus Christ, I will literally *die* if I see any more! *Literally*!" To be fair, that outburst would only be from the Gay groom. I'm not sure what a Lesbian bridezilla would do—maybe be smart enough to leave the shrieking to her Gay best man?

Of course, I couldn't sit by and do nothing as signs appeared all over LA exclaiming: "Save Marriage—Vote Yes On Prop 8!" As I drove to my job at *Will & Grace*, I stopped every fifty yards or so to rip up the signs and throw them in the back of my jeep for disposal later. I remember stopping at a red light, my jeep full of signs and the guy in the truck next to me giving me a thumbs up, as if to say, "Good job!" I returned the thumbs before I realized he thought I was putting the signs up. The "Yes on Prop 8!" sticker on his bumper as he pulled away confirmed that suspicion.

Earlier that year, the writers, cast, and some of the crew of *Will & Grace* had gone to New York to film some outdoor scenes. It was fun. Us writers got to spend a few days shooting in Central Park. It was an area I knew well, having spent some dirty, dirty time in the "rambles"—a very overgrown section of park by the lake where horny Gay men would gather to make a new friend or two. And tourists who sauntered in, enjoying the nature, were quickly seen rushing out, pale and shocked.

As I do whenever I traveled to New York, I sought out places that were important to me or had an impact on me when I lived there many years earlier .

My apartment on Thirteenth Street with the hordes of rats scattering as you came and went at night.

My other apartment on Thirteenth Street with the hordes of rats scattering as you came and went at night. Of course, New York had changed so much by then, the rats seemed to be of a higher class. They wore top hats and monocles.

The first Crunch Fitness on Thirteenth Street where I worked at the towel bar and stole money as I rented out towels—one dollar for me, one dollar for Crunch. I got fired when I asked my friend Tom to show me the Prince Albert he had literally just gotten, and the manager saw me give him towels to help stop the bleeding.

The too-numerous-to-see-in-one-trip restaurants I got fired from, including, Clair, which was on Seventh Avenue in Chelsea. No matter what fish my customers asked about, I used the description "mild, flakey white fish." The owner didn't like that.

CBGBs where, during a Suicidal Tendencies concert, I just peed on a wall because the men's room was so gross and it was so crowded anyway that no one would notice. It's a John Varvatos store now. That wall has a rack of $500 sweaters on it.

The Gay and Lesbian Center (currently known as The Lesbian, Gay, Bisexual & Transgender Community Center) where I walked the runway as Jackie Kennedy at a charity thing. I was so delighted that I had found the perfect knockoff pink Chanel suit and hat, it was almost a shame to put fake blood on it.

The apartment in Hell's kitchen that I shared with Heidi and Charlie, which used to be a funeral parlor. And possibly a porn store since, in the basement, we found hundreds of Beta videos with titles like *Batman and Throbbin* and *Giant Splash Shots 2*. We never did find *Shots 1*, but we didn't have a Beta video player so we didn't have to worry about coming late to that franchise.

Cooper Union, where ACT UP moved its meetings to when the number of members grew too much for the Center to hold. And where a relatively unknown Abraham Lincoln gave his "Right Makes Might" speech denouncing slavery.

The Village, where I patrolled with the Pink Panthers in an attempt to keep it safe. We had to change our T-shirts to read "Panther Patrol," when MGM found out and threatened to sue for copyright infringement.

But of course, the fun and fuzzy feeling of nostalgia eventually turns into the anger and sadness of memory.

Avenue A between Third and Fourth streets, where I got pushed into a bunch of garbage and called a "fag." I think one of the bags was full of diapers.

Avenue B and Tenth. Paul lived here—he's dead. He had a collection of Barbie dolls in their original boxes.

Avenue C and Fifth. Alejandro lived here—he's dead. I don't know if he collected anything.

The Cowgirl Hall of Fame restaurant, famous for serving an open bag of Fritos with chili plopped in it. Carlos was my waiter. We fooled around a few times, and I think we kind of liked each other. It was fun. He told me he was going away for a bit. After a week or so, I went to his restaurant with a few friends to get a bite to eat. When I asked our waiter when Carlos would be back, he told me he was dead, just as he put down our Frito-chili bag. Which, after a sad moment, we tore into. It was delicious. Call it grief-eating, but we ordered another one immediately.

The drugstore in the Village where Luis, dressed like a drag bunny on Easter, was harassed by some "bridge and tunnel" bros. They took off when Luis, in six-inch heels, led a charge of angry Gays back at them, screaming "These are our streets!"

The kiss-in at that straight bar.

The kiss-in at that other straight bar, where I remembered to bring ChapStick.

Taking over Grand Central Station, taking over St. Patrick's Cathedral, taking over the Holland Tunnel...all to raise awareness and protest government inaction.

The sidewalk where, over the years, that dead pigeon had been smashed into just another stain. The stain is still there, now so faded that it's only slightly darker than the surrounding asphalt

At some point after I got the job on *Will & Grace*, Heidi and Charlie flew to Los Angeles for a visit. Just a couple of years before, we were moving out of an apartment in the dead of night to avoid paying rent to a landlord we thought was sketchy, and now I was barking orders at a PA who came to take my coffee order, "Remember—an extra shot of espresso, one pump of chocolate!" We all had a really good laugh at that.

When Tracy and I were hired on the show, I was excited—I could finally get my Gay agenda across! And Tracy could too! She had other agendas but Gay was definitely one of them! And to millions of people! And get a check and free coffee too! Sweet!

We pitched a story about Will getting embarrassed by how "Gay" Jack was. Turns out it's hard to show things like inner homophobia in a twenty-two-minute sitcom. The word "fag" was said five times in the episode, and the network and sponsors were not happy with this attempt at a nuanced story of inner turmoil. "Will Works Out" became the "missing episode" and did not rerun for many, many years. Lesson learned.

Activism can mean many different things at different times.

So, I said "Um, Yes" at the San Francisco City Hall that day. It helped that the overexcited clerk also told us that Harvey Milk had been assassinated where we were standing.[59] I told myself we were also honoring him. It's a bit suspect that Harvey died on the exact same spot where Marilyn married Joe, though I did catch the faintest wisp of Chanel No. 5, a favorite of both Marilyn and Harvey.

"Do you have the rings?" When the clerk learned we did not, she looked as if she might cry, her perfect moment ruined. To assuage her tears, I quickly fashioned my Starbucks straw into a ring that we took turns putting on each other. And it may have been the fact that I was over-caffeinated, but my heart did feel some kind of something—not something holy, but maybe empowering.

Of course, they will come for same-sex marriage again. But this time, I will defend it without hesitation. To show our support, Chris and I will just get divorced and marry again. I'll make sure to do it around Chris's birthday and to stop for coffee first.

---

59 Harvey Milk was the first openly Gay politician to be elected to public office. He sponsored a bill banning discrimination based on sexual orientation in public accommodations, housing, and employment. He was assassinated by the one man who voted against it.

Acknowledgments

A very special thank you to my literary agent, Lisa Hagan for her hard work and amazing-ness.

The acquiring editor, Debra Englander, for seeing something in my stories and thinking others should too.

My managing editor, Caitlin Burdette for her sick editorial skills and guidance.

My publicist, Michele Karlsberg, for going above and beyond. I'm grateful AF.

Thank you: Tracy Poust, Luis José Salazar, Charlie Welch, Heidi Dorow, Amy Engelberg, Max Mutchnick, David Kohan, Michael Patrick King, Ron Medici, Blair Fell, Ted Ottaviano, Helen Keller, John O'Brien, Queer Action Figures, Tom Hill, Laura Kightlinger, Garrett Sutton, Corey Rubin, ACT UP NY, the Latina/o Caucus of ACT UP NY, Ryan O'Connell, the man on the box of Doan's Pills, and my parents, Jack and Eleanor.

And of course Chris Young and all of our cats: Maggie, Chaos (thank you, Debbie Harry!), Kitty (Dr. Katherine Louise Bellows), Fred, Simon, Maria, Howard Bannister, and Elliot.

And our tortoises: Wentworth and Boris.

And our rabbit, Ramen.

And our beagle, Daisy.
All of whom made me whatever I am today.

About the Author

photo credit: Chris Young

Jon Kinnally was born in Syracuse, New York and went to college at Oswego State before moving to a then-affordable Manhattan where he pursued acting and performed with his writing partner, Tracy Poust, in their comedy group Loud Blouse.

After relocating to Los Angeles, they got a job on a new show called Will & Grace and stayed with it for it's entire eight seasons, eventually running it and returning for the reboot. Over the years, there were many Emmy nominations as well as a Writers Guild Award for Outstanding Writing in Episodic Comedy in 2018.

He has also worked on several other shows with Tracy, including Ugly Betty—Emmy and NAACP award nominations—

and The Crazy Ones which they ran and had the privilege to write for the great Robin Williams.

He currently lives in Spain with his husband, Chris, and their cats, Howard Bannister and Elliott.

To find out more, visit jonkinnally.com or @jonkinnally on Instagram.